Drawing and Designing with Confidence

Drawing and Designing with Confidence
A Step-By-Step Guide

Mike W. Lin, ASLA

VNR VAN NOSTRAND REINHOLD
New York

Copyright © 1993 Van Nostrand Reinhold
I(T)P ™ A division of International Thomson Publishing Inc.
The ITP logo is a trademark under license

Printed in Hong Kong
For more information, contact:

Van Nostrand Reinhold
115 Fifth Avenue
New York, NY 10003

International Thomson Publishing GmbH
Königswinterer Strasse 418
53227 Bonn
Germany

International Thomson Publishing Europe
Berkshire House 168–173
High Holborn
London WC1V 7AA
England

International Thomson Publishing Asia
221 Henderson Road #05 10
Henderson Building
Singapore 0315

Thomas Nelson Australia
102 Dodds Street
South Melbourne, 3205
Victoria, Australia

International Thomson Publishing Japan
Hirakawacho Kyowa Building, 3F
2-2-1 Hirakawacho
Chiyoda-ku, 102 Tokyo
Japan

Nelson Canada
1120 Birchmount Road
Scarborough, Ontario
Canada M1K 5G4

International Thomson Editores
Campos Eliseos 385, Piso 7
Col. Polanco
11560 Mexico D.F. Mexico

96 97 98 99 CP 10 9 8 7 6 5 4

Library of Congress Cataloging-in-Publication Data

Lin, Mike W.
   Drawing and designing with confidence/Mike W. Lin.
      p.   cm.
   Includes bibliographical references and index.
   ISBN 0-442-00176-2
   1. Architectural drawing—Technique.   2. Architectural design—
Technique.   I. Title.
NA2708.L56   1992
720'.28'4—dc20   91-41427
                                                      CIP

To JoAnn, Brian, and Sharon with love

CONTENTS

PREFACE

Are you afraid of drawing or hesitant to try? It is my goal to provide a step-by-step method for achieving good graphics as well as good design skills. This book is for practitioners at all levels, from beginners and students to teachers and professionals in all the design disciplines.

In chapter 1, "loose-vs-tight" concepts illustrate that with the right attitude anyone can break mental blocks and draw well. It also shows how to activate the right side of the brain and to discover artistic skill buried within you. Forty-five fundamental principles of good graphics are outlined and discussed in chapter 2. If studied carefully, they will help you to make fewer drawing mistakes and, regardless of talent, to draw better and with confidence.

The heart of the book is the exploration of rendering techniques and types in chapters 3 and 4. Twenty techniques and eight types are explained and illustrated. A media matrix serves as a cross reference between the two groups. Analyzing the matrix helps to familiarize you with the relationships between technique and appropriate media, to enable you to use them to their fullest advantage. Chapter 5 focuses on lettering, both in pencil and marker.

Various elements that are important in creating interest and realism in a drawing are known as entourage, and this is the subject of chapter 6. People, vegetation, cars, furniture, skies, water, glass, and other details bring a drawing to life. After studying entourage, the reader will be prepared to understand and construct perspective drawings (chap. 7). Emphasis is placed on quick and simple methods in one- and two-point perspective, and the use of a perspective chart. Once the basic principles of perspective have been understood, readers will be able to sketch with greater confidence and success (chap. 8).

The design process is approached in chapter 9 through step-by-step procedures that lead toward a successful design solution. Six basic design forms and their twenty-three design principles are included.

Finally, the appendices include useful information on time-saving techniques as well as recommendations for model materials, for drawing paper and boards, and for a list of markers.

The Chinese character at the beginning of each chapter means "eternity" or "forever." It is a reminder to the reader to be loose and not afraid to try. After all, your drawing can never get worse: it can only improve by trying without fear. You will be glad you did.

Remember, the more you draw, the more mistakes you will make, the more principles you will learn, and the more success you will gain. Therefore, you will gain more confidence; once you have got the confidence, you can draw and do anything.

ACKNOWLEDGMENTS

The book I have always dreamed of writing has at last become a reality. Its final form is thanks to a team of dedicated architects, landscape architects, interior designers, and illustrators who spent valuable time and effort in assisting me: Stephen Clay, Michelle Flynn, Debbie P. Graviss, Shannon Gordon, Roger Greidanus, Christine Hess, Audrey Hyde, Kevin Marshall, Chad Moor, Russ Richey, and Cara Silliman.

Special thanks go to those individuals who contributed drawings they completed during one of my graphics workshops in Manhattan, Kansas, and to the professionals who very generously contributed their works. Without such a variety in the content, this book may not have had the quality and diversity needed for academia and the design professions.

Thanks are also extended to the thousands of participants in my workshops who inspired me to write this book. Many have shared their expertise and helped to enrich the content of the book.

Special acknowledgment goes to the American Society of Landscape Architects, American Institute of Architects, American Institute of Architecture Students, American Society of Interior Designers, American Institute of Building Designers, and Associate Landscape Contractors of America. Together with many of their regional chapters, they have sponsored workshops and seminars across the country that have helped me shape this book. Also, thanks go to the staff at Van Nostrand Reinhold. It was a pleasure working with them on my previous book, *Architectural Rendering Techniques: A Color Reference*, and it is good to have such a valuable team back on this book.

Most of all, I extended by deepest gratitude to my beloved wife JoAnn, who has supported me in the last twenty years and who stands beside me whenever I need her. I am also grateful to my son Brian for his assistance in many of my career endeavors, and to my lovely daughter Sharon for her refreshing sparkle and charm.

1. 永 LOOSE VS TIGHT

What does it take to draw and design well? Maybe one needs to be talented, but there is much more to it than that. Attitude plays a big part, along with confidence and a willingness to take risks.

A good attitude will help you in whatever you do. This means sharing with others, taking initiative, taking risks, being energetic, believing in and liking yourself, and listening to others. Having a good attitude will help you to loosen up and be receptive, instead of being tight and afraid to try.

Loose vs tight means a willingness to try instead of being afraid to start. A tight person is handicapped with fear and does not want to take risks or make mistakes. It is this fear that keeps a tight person from starting and just jumping into a drawing. Being loose has to do with attitude. It is hard to be loose without having confidence in your work and yourself. You must genuinely like what you do and convey that positive feeling to others. *You* are the only one who can keep yourself from drawing well. One gifted with talent will not necessarily be successful without discipline. Also, people are not always born with talent; in fact, with hard work, any person can be talented.

When you draw, go ahead and take risks. Don't be afraid to make mistakes. Try to see a mistake as something positive. A great artist can turn any mistake into part of the drawing. Always have confidence in your work, and this will enable you to take criticism in a positive way. Know that criticism could lead to better ideas. Loose people don't worry about what others think about their drawing, but they do listen to others to pick up ideas that are informative.

RIGHT BRAIN AND LEFT BRAIN

In order to draw well, one must use the correct side of the brain. The human brain has a right- and a left-side mode (fig. 1-1). The left-side mode is "right handed"—it is sensible, tight, non-risk-taking, analytical, and it comprehends facts. It is this side of the brain that produces tight characteristics. The right-side mode is "left handed"—it is artistic, flexible, loose, risk-taking, intuitive, and it perceives objects as they actually are as opposed to seeing mere symbols as the left brain does. Generally, society gears us to use the left side of our brains. The techniques covered in this book will assist you in using the right side of your brain.

When a person is being creative, he is simultaneously using both sides of the brain. Simple exercises can help you to stimulate the right side of your brain. They are difficult in the beginning, because you are trying to balance both sides of the brain and not allow the left side to be dominant.

- Place both of your hands in front of you and extend the index finger on each. Rotate your arms in opposite directions (fig. 1-2).

- Pat your head with one hand, and at the same time rub your stomach in a circular motion with the other hand. Then, quickly switch actions, patting your stomach and rubbing your head.

HOW TO IMPROVE GRAPHICS

Good graphics, like many other skills, require strong personal discipline and commitment. If applied properly, the following directives will help to improve your drawing skills.

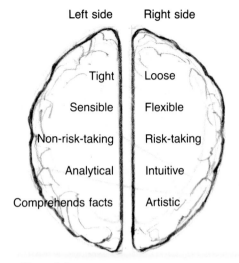

Left side	Right side
Tight	Loose
Sensible	Flexible
Non-risk-taking	Risk-taking
Analytical	Intuitive
Comprehends facts	Artistic

Figure 1-1.

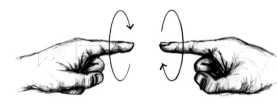

Figure 1-2.

- **Observation.** Study the graphics in magazines, books, and art exhibits. This will help reinforce what you know and give you incentive to produce quality work.
- **Demonstration.** Take every available opportunity to watch how other people draw. This is particularly important because it shows the actual process of drawing, alleviates curiosity behind a good drawing, and helps create self-confidence.
- **Collection.** Collect graphic reference books and look for good graphics examples; sort them into files for tracing and generating ideas.

- **Imitation.** Recognize good graphics, and imitate them. This will help to refine your drawing skills. Be careful not to allow imitation to develop into a crutch.
- **Confidence.** Never become discouraged. Confidence in yourself is half the battle. The more confidence you are able to gain, the more productive you will be, and the more you can learn and progress. Tell yourself that you can do it.
- **Creativity.** Think and draw creatively at all times. Creativity often means simply doing something in a new or unconventional way. Look for things you've never noticed before.
- **Looseness.** Don't be afraid of making mistakes or taking risks. Risk-taking is the only way to learn and progress. Start with a positive attitude and overcome hesitation. When a mistake occurs, say "I like it" and turn that mistake into a good part of the drawing.
- **Practice.** Improvement without practice is impossible, so practice drawing constantly.
- **Persistence.** You must persevere to produce good graphics. Every effort, even if it is a single dot or line, is important to achieve a great drawing. Often the last minutes of execution in a drawing will make the difference. Never give up, even in the face of opposition. Remember, you can never get any worse, only better, and you will never realize your capabilities unless you push to reach your full potential.
- **Criticism.** Ask knowledgeable people in related subject areas to criticize your work. Without criticism, you will repeat your mistakes again and again. Accept constructive criticism as a positive part of the process.
- **Improvement.** Always attempt to improve your abilities and increase your understanding. Improving depends on

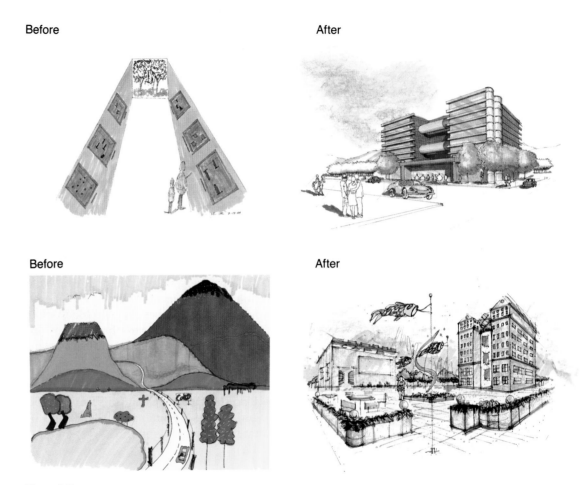

Before
After
Before
After

Figure 1-3. Top: Nancy Eletto, Bottom: Martha Lent, participants, ML Graphic Workshop.

constant practice and constructive criticism, as well as reaching beyond yourself.

• **Sharing.** When you share and verbalize your knowledge to others, you actually educate yourself twice. What you know will be reinforced and further clarified.

The following are examples of loose-vs-tight drawings (fig. 1-3, previous page). These "before" and "after" perspectives were each completed in one to two hours. The "before" drawings were done by students before they learned the techniques taught in this book. The "after" drawings were done after a week to ten days of instruction in the techniques explained in the following chapters.

The twelve blocks (fig. 1-4) are also used to show improvement from before to after. The first four blocks on the left are examples of the same drawing reproduced and rendered in different media: pencil, colored pencil, marker, and pastel. Each block was done in six minutes. The middle blocks were done in a total of 40 minutes. The student was told to design a courtyard. The first block is used for creating a bubble diagram. The second is the plan of the courtyard. The last two blocks are a section and perspective of the design. The right four blocks illustrate the elements of people, trees, hands, perspective, and lettering. They were done in three to five minutes each.

The last drawing (fig. 1-5) is a good example of what the twelve blocks should look like after learning all the techniques taught in this book.

Figure 1-4. Jodi Hinzmann, participant, ML Graphic Workshop.

Before

After

Figure 1-5. Steve Allenstein, participant, ML Graphic Workshop.

2. 永 PRINCIPLES OF GOOD GRAPHICS

This chapter presents forty-five principles to consider in order to produce high-quality graphics. If remembered and practiced, these essential principles can assure an artist of excellence. Some are obvious, while others may be based on concepts not easily understood. Study each of these principles thoroughly and apply them to your drawings. Review them as you work until they become fully integrated with your approach to drawing. They will help to stimulate the right side of your brain and to make you more creative.

The forty-five principles of good graphics are divided into three categories: line, composition, and color. These principles are discussed in depth in the section that follows and summarized in the list below. Also see figure 2-1.

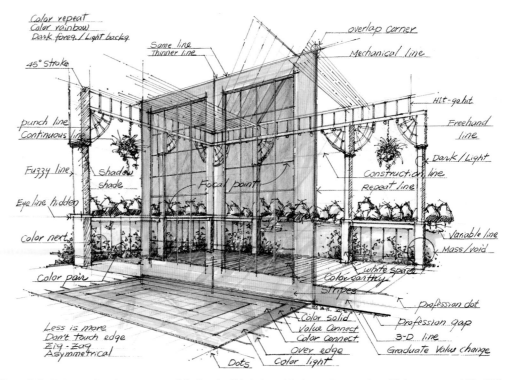

Figure 2-1. Rebecca Smith, participant, ML Graphic Workshop. Marker, color pencil, and felt-tip pen on 19″ × 24″ marker paper. 1 hour.

FORTY-FIVE PRINCIPLES OF GRAPHICS

Line
1. Chisel the Point
2. Fuzzy Line
3. Hit-Go-Hit
4. Professional Gap
5. Professional Dot
6. Overlap Corner
7. Mechanical Line
8. Freehand Line
9. Construction Line
10. Continuous Line
11. Repeat Line
12. Variable Line
13. Same Line
14. Thinner Line
15. Punch Line
16. 3-D Line
17. Thin/Thick
18. Thick Stroke
19. 45-Degree Stroke
20. Gradual Value Change
21. Over Edge
22. Stripes
23. Dots

Composition
24. Start Small
25. Less is More
26. Don't Touch Edges
27. White Space
28. Zig-Zag
29. Dark/Light
30. Mass/Void
31. Value Connect
32. Shade and Shadow
33. Asymmetrical
34. Eye Line Hidden
35. Focal Point
36. Dark Foreground/Light Background

Color
37. Color Wheel
38. Color Pair
39. Color Next
40. Color Rainbow
41. Color Repeat
42. Color Light
43. Color Solid
44. Color Connect
45. Color Earthy

LINE

1. Chisel the Point

Shaping the pencil point by rubbing it back and forth in short strokes on the page is a fundamental step in creating many line qualities in a drawing, such as fuzzy line, hit-go-hit, and freehand line.

HOW: Hold the pencil as you would to draw, and chisel the point on the paper by rubbing it back and forth to achieve a wide, flat edge. Keep the pencil at an angle close to the paper for a wider stroke. A soft pencil lead such as No. 6B will provide the fuzzier, wider line needed in good drawings.

2. Fuzzy Line

A fuzzy line has soft edges and is a light and delicate rather than a hard, definite line. There are no lines or outlines in real objects. When a drawing is completed, the fuzzy line will become part of the object itself. It is used to draw man-made objects such as buildings and cars.

HOW: Chisel the pencil to make a wide point; then use consistent pressure and draw a line of the same thickness.

3. Hit-Go-Hit

A fuzzy line drawn with distinct beginning and ending segments helps to develop interest and depth within a drawing. Applying hit allows the designer to pause a moment before drawing the line.

HOW: Chisel the point and draw the beginning of the line about ⅛ to ¼ inch long, go back and forth a few times, then draw a fuzzy line. End the line using the same method as at the beginning.

4. Professional Gap

A small break in a line, a "professional" gap, helps to simulate light reflecting off an object. It also provides for easy transition when drawing curves or long lines.

HOW: Draw a fuzzy or hit-go-hit line, leaving an occasional gap 1/16 inch to ⅛ inch wide.

5. Professional Dot

A "professional" dot is a point after a line. It occurs as a result of fast drawing, adding movement and life, and providing the finishing touch, like a period at the end of a sentence.

HOW: Draw a fuzzy or hit-go-hit line quickly, then add a small dot, with a gap in between the two. After a while, with practice, this will occur naturally as you draw quickly.

6. Overlap Corner

Lines that intersect at the corner make objects appear more square, sharp, and complete. The overlap corner is quicker than drawing a corner with lines abutting perfectly. It gives the drawing a loose and professional look.

HOW: Intersect two fuzzy or two hit-go-hit lines at the corner, ⅛ inch to ¼ inch in length, depending on the size of the object. Use a small overlap for refined drawings and long overlap for loose drawings.

7. Mechanical Line

A mechanical line is a clean, crisp line drawn with a straightedge. It is quicker, more consistent, and more accurate than a line drawn freehand. It also allows you to draw a long line easily.

HOW: Use a straightedge and apply fuzzy or hit-go-hit line, overlap corner, professional gap, and professional dot. These combinations make hard lines look loose.

8. Freehand Line

A freehand line is simply a line drawn without a straightedge. It is soft and organic, and can be used to sketch small-scale drawings quickly. It allows you to be more creative than when using a straightedge and stimulates the right brain. However, it takes more time to draw than the mechanical line.

HOW: Chisel the point; then use the fuzzy line, hit-go-hit, continuous line, professional dot, and professional gap to draw freehand lines.

9. Construction Line

A construction line is a light, thin, fuzzy line used to plot out the preliminary drawing. It is a safe way to establish an overall view of the drawing without commiting to placement. These lines can be changed or erased easily.

HOW: Use fuzzy lines with very light pressure to sketch the overall composition of your drawing.

10. Continuous Line
A continuous line is a single, nonstop, quickly drawn line that captures the essence of the subject.

HOW: Using a fuzzy line and hit-go-hit line, draw continuously without lifting the pencil from the paper.

11. Repeat Line
A repeat line is simply a line that echoes the main lines of a drawing. Repeat lines give an object a three-dimensional look by adding depth; they help stimulate creativity and looseness.

HOW: Loosely repeat fuzzy lines or construction lines two or more times over the edges of an object. Apply more repeat lines to the shaded side of an object.

12. Variable Line
A variable line is a fuzzy line that varies in thickness. It gives a drawing a three-

dimensional, realistic look and is used to draw people, trees, and other living beings.

HOW: Chisel the point, twist the pencil, and apply varied pressure to create different thicknesses of line. Where light hits on an object, the line becomes thinner or lighter than in shadow, where the line should thicken or become darker.

13. Same Line
A "same" line is one that is of even thickness and darkness throughout. There are no lines in our surroundings, therefore using the same line weight will allow a drawing to achieve a more realistic appearance.

HOW: Select a line weight and apply it throughout the drawing. Sometimes it is necessary to use different line weights to differentiate distances from the observer. In this case, use a sequential line weight, using the thinnest line for objects farthest from the viewer, a medium line for the middle ground, and a heavy line for the foreground. The bigger a drawing, the thicker the line that may be applied to achieve readability, although this does not necessarily provide a better quality drawing.

14. Thinner Line
Use of thin, lightweight lines throughout a drawing gives it a soft, often lifelike appearance. Heavier lines are sometimes used to create a bigger drawing, however, because they are easy to read.

HOW: Apply thin lines throughout the drawing. The line weight used will depend upon the size of the drawing and the detail required.

15. Punch Line
A punch line, also known as a profile line, is is a slightly heavier line used to outline an object that is not well defined. Because it gives a bold, loose appearance, it is not used in refined work. However, it can be used on plan, elevation, and section drawings.

HOW: Use the same line weight throughout the drawing, then use a heavier line weight to outline the object that you want to define.

16. 3-D Line
Thick and thin lines next to each other are together known as a 3-D line; they can create a three-dimensional look or fuzzy line image, and add quality to a drawing.

HOW: Outline first with a thick line, then with a thin line, leaving a space between them of about $\frac{1}{16}$ inch to $\frac{1}{8}$ inch, depending upon the size of the object.

17. Thin/Thick Strokes
The outline of an object is usually thin but dark enough to control the tone line used inside the object. Tone lines are thicker and lighter than the outline line.

HOW: Lightly chisel the point and draw the outline of the object with a thin line using firm pressure (use fuzzy line, hit-go-hit, and overlap corner techniques). Then chisel the point further to create a wide stroke and apply tone lines with less pressure inside the object. The tone lines should have consistent thickness; do not use hit-go-hit strokes to avoid a pipelike appearance.

18. Thick Strokes
Use thick fuzzy lines to create toned surfaces. Thick strokes help to complete a drawing quickly and create a smooth tone effect.

HOW: Chisel the pencil to its widest point and draw. Soft-lead pencils such as 6B are recommended.

19. 45-Degree Stroke
A series of parallel fuzzy lines that are about 45 degrees to the edge of the page are easy and quick to draw. They create consistency and a sleek appearance in a drawing.

HOW: Draw from top to bottom only, allowing the pencil to slide lightly when returning to the top of the next line. Do not draw back and forth.

20. Gradual Value Change
Light reflection causes a gradual value change in every object. Although the human eye does not immediately perceive gradual value change, it must be created in the drawing for a more realistic look.

HOW: Chisel the point and use a 45-degree stroke to draw tone lines from left to right, while gradually reducing pressure from dark to light. (A left-handed person should draw lines from right to left.) Always allow the strokes to touch each other, leaving a gap occasionally to suggest the 45-degree angle.

21. Over Edge
In the over-edge technique, while applying a gradual value change to an object, allow some of the lines to overlap the edge of the object slightly. This creates a soft, loose effect.

HOW: When applying value to an object, intentionally overlap the edge with some of the strokes. How much overlap depends upon the refinement of the drawing.

22. Stripes
Stripes are used to create interest, depth, and movement, and to show shadow patterns and angles of slope. Stripes also give the drawing a slick appearance.

HOW: Use any medium and add stripes randomly at any angle.

23. Dots
Dots create texture and detail and can be used to create gradual value change.

HOW: Using an appropriate line weight, hold the pen/pencil vertically to avoid dragging, apply dots randomly.

COMPOSITION
24. Start Small
Starting a drawing on a small scale, a thumbnail sketch, enables you to study the overall value and composition easily. A small sketch also takes less time to complete than larger formats and allows you to work out problems that might ruin a large drawing.

HOW: Begin with a sheet of paper no larger than 8½ by 11 inches. Complete a single drawing which you can use as a study drawing or can enlarge to any desired size for other purposes.

25. Less is More
Often when too much time is spent on a drawing, it becomes overworked and loses

one of the most important principles of graphics: white space. Applying less time may produce a better drawing.

HOW: Allow yourself a limited time to spend on a drawing, and when the time is up, stop. Remember, you can never do a "perfect" drawing no matter how much time you allow; even the best drawing will have room for improvement.

26. Don't Touch Edges
Be careful not to let lines touch the edges of the paper, and leave a white border along the edge of a drawing. This helps to assure sufficient white space and to create a good zig-zag composition. The don't-touch-edges treatment gives the drawing a framed effect, a principle that applies to framing a picture.

HOW: Allow ½ inch to 4 inches of white space along the edge of the paper, depending upon the size of the drawing and the composition.

27. White Space
White space is one of the most important elements in a drawing, because it contributes to zig-zag (28) and mass/void (30). The human eye, upon opening, sees white before black. Therefore, leaving white space will attract attention to a drawing.

HOW: Place a "W" in areas to be left white or a light value; this serves as a reminder when rendering. Also limit the time spent to avoid overworking. White space does not necessarily have to be pure white; it can also be a light value of any color.

28. Zig-Zag
In a zig-zag composition the four edges of a drawing do not assume a regular geometrical shape such as a square, triangle, or circle. Establishing a zig-zag creates variety and realism.

HOW: To break the geometrical shape, strategically place details such as furniture, flags, fountains, plants, people, trees, benches, and cars in the drawing to create zig-zag or uneven edges by jutting out or moving in.

29. Dark/Light
Dark/Light is used to give the subject of a drawing, such as the corner of a building, a dark value on one side and a light one on the other side. This creates a three-dimensional image.

HOW: At the corner of a subject, make one side (the smaller or shady side, away from the drawing's light source) at least twice as dark as the other side (the larger or lighter side). This must be applied consistently

throughout the drawing according to the position and quality of the light source.

30. Mass/Void
We identify objects in the environment by their shapes, and by the different values of one next to the other: for example, dark grass next to a light road, or a dark building against a light sky. Proper use of this principle of mass (dark) to void (light) helps to clarify different materials in the drawing.

HOW: When materials change in a drawing, apply a dark value on dark material (mass) and a light value on the light material (void). For example, a dark building (mass) should be placed next to a light sky (void), and dark grass (mass) should be next to a light road (void). This helps to identify the different materials and to create a good zig-zag composition.

31. Value Connect
If the contrast of mass to void is too great, a spotty appearance is created. Value connect corrects this by joining the dark and light values with a medium tone.

HOW: Study the arrangement of values assigned to each subject in the drawing to make certain that no very dark and very light values are next to each other.

32. Shade and Shadow

Shade and shadow provide punch, depth, and realism, and make a drawing more readable.

HOW: Shadow only occurs on surfaces that receive a light source, and never on the shade side. The more recessed an object, the greater the shadow received. Double the value from sunny to shade surface, and from shade to shadow surface in order to achieve a three-dimensional appearance of an object.

33. Asymmetrical

An asymmetrical composition creates interest and excitement, establishing a realistic setting and avoiding monotony.

HOW: Use different elements such as people, vegetation, cars, or furniture to achieve an asymmetrical balance and create visual harmony and value balance. Avoid symmetrical placement of objects.

34. Eye Line Hidden

Generally speaking one can never see the eye line (horizon line), unless overlooking the ocean or a large lake. Therefore hiding the eye line can make the drawing more realistic and pleasing to the eye.

HOW: Obscure the eye line with entourage such as people, trees, cars, mountains, or buildings.

35. Focal Point

The center of the drawing is the focal point to which your eyes are usually drawn. This is not necessarily at the physical center of the page.

HOW: Provide more detail and darker values to the important part, the focal point, of the drawing, still allowing white space within. This method is used when less time is available to spend on a drawing; in other cases the dark foreground/light background method is used (see below).

36. Dark Foreground/Light Background

In nature, objects appear to be darkest nearest the viewer and lightest farthest away, in the background. There is a gradation of values from foreground to background.

HOW: When rendering, use light colors in the background, gradually darkening them toward the foreground. This method takes time to complete and is best applied to refined drawings.

COLOR

37. Color Wheel

A color wheel contains three primary colors (yellow, blue, and red) and three secondary colors (green, purple, and orange). The secondary colors come from mixtures of the primary colors. When spinning the color wheel, one sees white. When all the colors on the wheel are mixed, brown or black is produced.

38. Color Pair

The human eye is like a camera. When looking at a color, we search out its opposite color in the color wheel: red and green, blue and orange, purple and yellow. These color combinations are known as complementary colors or color pairs.

When a color pair is used, the two colors adjacent but unmixed excite each other; when mixed, they create an earthy tone.

HOW: When rendering, add to a main color a small amount of its complementary: red to green grass and trees, for example, or orange to blue sky, or yellow to a purple carpet. An easy way to remember the color pair is to apply the primary colors to three fingertips. When any of the two fingers are put together, the color they create is the color pair to the color on the finger remaining. Another easy way to remember color pair is to associate red and green with Christmas, blue and orange with the sunset, and yellow and purple with the iris.

39. Color Next

Color next is the use of three sequential colors from the color wheel. It creates harmony and gradual value change, and is pleasing to the eye.

HOW: According to the color wheel, use groups of three consecutive colors. For example, the color next of a tree will contain yellow, green, and blue, while its color pair is red. Therefore, all the above colors shall be included when rendering a tree.

40. Color Rainbow

Rainbow colors create interest, excitement, and color in a drawing, thus avoiding monotony.

HOW: Include at least six dominant colors from the color wheel and two to three shades from each color. This technique will encompass most of the previous color principles. Use the color repeat discussed below to achieve a quality drawing.

41. Color Repeat

Because colors bounce back and forth, objects in the environment receive all seven colors in the spectrum: For example, a tree contains all colors, but green is most dominant. Once a color is used, it must be applied throughout the entire drawing. This is known as color repeat; it produces a more realistic and pleasing effect since it is the way we actually see.

HOW: Once a color is used, repeat it on every object in the drawing, making sure to establish dominance: more green on trees, more red on brick, more blue in the sky, and so on.

42. Color Light

Color light means working from light to dark in a drawing. The human eye is generally likely to see light color, first, making the use of color light a good way for the beginner to work.

HOW: Apply the lightest colors first throughout the drawing. Gradually build up to the darkest colors.

43. Color Solid

Color solid is similar to "paint-by-numbers," but when combined with the principles of gradual value change and stripes, color solid creates a smooth, sleek look and avoids spottiness. This method can also produce mass/void in a drawing.

HOW: Apply color to an entire area, such as grass, carpet, or building, while still main-taining some white space and gradual value change. Remember to use color pair to create excitement.

44. Color Connect

Too much white space between colored objects can create spottiness. Color connect pulls a drawing together with tints and intermediate colors in some of the white spaces.

HOW: If possible, do not allow white space to surround an object completely. Use a light color in white space to connect two objects: for example, color the road light gray to connect the grass on both sides.

45. Color Earthy

Our eyes search for the opposite color on the color pair. When we see green, we subconsciously see red. When we see light or white, we therefore see dark or black. Hence, if there is an existence of light, an earthy tone of that color is needed in the drawing in order to represent the way we see.

HOW: Shade the object with black or mix the color pair to create an earthy tone. Outlining the drawing with brown or black will also provide the drawing with definition and uniformity. A bright green tree can be toned down with black or red, and can also be outlined with black.

EXAMPLES

In the drawings of a shed (fig. 2-2) the forty-five principles of graphics are successfully applied. The same subject is repeated in each sketch with a different combination of these principles to make the drawing more effective.

The sketches of a barn (fig. 2-3) illustrate a comparison study of good and bad graphics. Use of the forty-five principles will allow you to make fewer mistakes, saving time and enhancing your drawing quality.

The following (figs. 2-4 and 2-5) is a comparison study of similar spaces drawn and designed either poorly or nicely. Accompanying the drawings are comments explaining what is wrong and right and what can be done to improve them. It is evident that if you can draw well, you can most likely design well. So, be loose, practice, and draw, draw, draw!

Following are eight sets of before/after drawings (figs. 2-6 and 2-7) done by participants who attended the author's graphic workshop in Manhattan, Kansas. The before drawing was drawn in one hour when the participant first arrived. The after drawing was completed in between one to three hours (including designing time), after the participant had studied all the principles of good graphics for a period of 6 to 10 days. The dramatic improvement is proof that *anyone,* regardless of "talent" or skill, with knowledge of the principles in this book, can draw well.

The additional samples demonstrate various types of drawings using different principles of graphics (figs. 2-8 to 2-12).

Figure 2-2 Travis Rice, participant, ML Graphic Workshop. Pencil and colored pencil on 5″ × 7″ sketch paper each. 5 to 15 minutes each.

Missing: Professional gap, professional dot, overlap corner, and variable line.

Missing: Focal point, fuzzy line, and too spotty.

Good use of: Fuzzy line, hit-go-hit, professional gap, professional dot, and overlap corner.

Missing: White space, zig-zag, and don't touch edges.

Missing: Hit-go-hit, 45-degree stroke, and too spotty.

Good use of: 45-degree stroke, gradual value change, zig-zag, focal point, and mass/void.

Missing: White space, color rainbow, and color light.

Missing: Color next, color rainbow, and color earthy.

Good use of: Color pair, color next, color rainbow, color repeat, and color earthy.

Figure 2-3 Studies that demonstrate the importance of the forty-five principles.

After

Before

Before   After

Figure 2-4 (Top) CRIT: After: Good use of mechanical line, zig-zag, value connect, eye line hidden, color pair, and color earthy. Before: Missing gradual value change, zig-zag, mass/void, and color rainbow, poor figures, and eye line is showing.

(Bottom) CRIT: After: Good use of mechanical line, same line, dots, asymmetrical, and color earthy. Before: Missing gradual value change, zig-zag and mass/void, too spotty, poor figures, and eye line is showing.

After drawings: Chad Moor, participant, ML Graphic Workshop; before drawings: participants' first day, ML Graphic Workshop. Marker, colored pencil, and felt-tip pen on 19″ × 24″ marker paper each. 1 to 3 hours each.

After

Before

Before

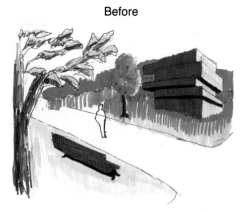

After

Figure 2-5. (Top) CRIT: After: Good use of mechanical line, gradual value change, stripes, zig-zag, shade and shadow, focal point, and color rainbow. Before: Missing gradual value change, zig-zag, shade and shadow, focal point, color rainbow, and color light.

(Bottom) CRIT: After: Good use of stripes, zig-zag, asymmetrical, eye line hidden,

dark foreground/light background, color pair. Before: Missing focal point, color pair, color rainbow, color repeat and color connect; no black outline and touch edges.

After drawings: Chad Moor, participant, ML Graphic Workshop; before drawings: participants' first day, ML Graphic Workshop. Marker, colored pencil, and felt-tip pen on 19″ × 24″ marker paper each. 1 to 3 hours each.

After

Before

Before

After

Figure 2-6. (Top) CRIT: After: Good use of professional gap, don't touch the edges, zig-zag, color rainbow, color repeat, and color light. Before: Missing gradual value change, same line, zig-zag, and focal point; too spotty and touch the edges.

(Bottom) CRIT: After: Good use of overlap corner, gradual value change, start light, zig-zag, focal point, and color pair. Before: Missing thinner line, start small, white space,

mass/void, and focal point; poor figures.

Top: Jeff Kerr, before drawing: first day, 1 hour; after drawing: eighth day, 2 hours. Bottom: Norma Pinette, before drawing: first day, 1 hour; after drawing: fifth day, 2 hours. Participants, ML Graphic Workshop. Marker, colored pencil, and felt-tip pen on 19″ × 24″ marker paper each.

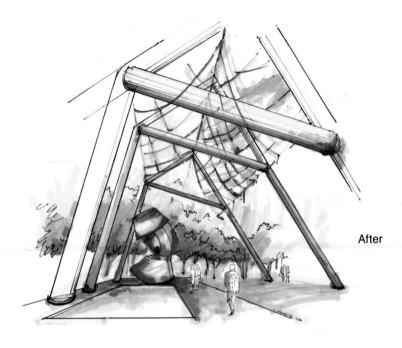

After

Before

Before

After

Figure 2-7. (Top) CRIT: After: Good use of mechanical line, punch line, gradual value change, focal point, color pair, and color light. Before: Missing zig-zag, color rainbow, color repeat, and black outline; poor figures.

(Bottom) CRIT: After: Good use of freehand line, stripes, white space, mass/void, color pair, and color connect. Before: Missing start small, zig-zag, mass/void, focal point, black outlined, and has touched the edges.

Top: Curt Arnette, before: first day, 1 hour; after drawing: fifth day, 1 hour. Bottom: Mike Tanzini, before drawing: first day, 1 hour; after drawing: tenth day, 4 hours. Participants, ML Graphic Workshop. Marker, colored pencil, and felt-tip pen on 19″ × 24″ marker paper each.

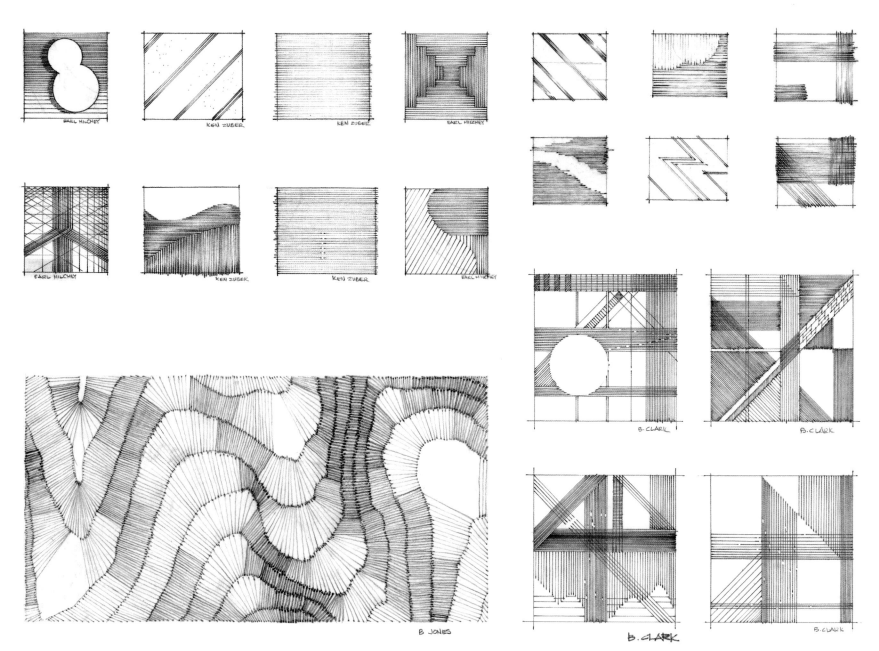

Figure 2-8. B. Jones, B. Clark, Earl Hilchey, Ken Zuber, participants, ML Graphic Workshop. Pencil on 16" × 20" sketch paper. 2 hours.

Figure 2-9. Top left: Robert Boulton, St. Louis, MO. Pencil on 6″ × 6″ tracing paper. 2 hours. Right and bottom: participants, ML Graphic Workshop. Pencil and black China marker on 6″ × 12″ sketch paper each. 2 minutes to 1 hour each.

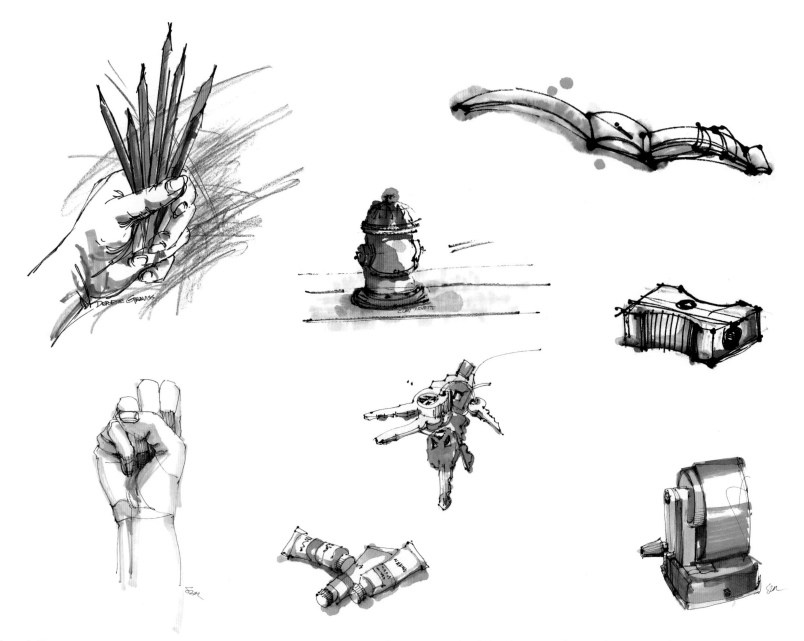

Figure 2-10. Participants, ML Graphic Workshop. Marker, colored pencil, pastel, and felt-tip pen on 6″ × 8″ sketch paper each. 3 to 10 minutes each.

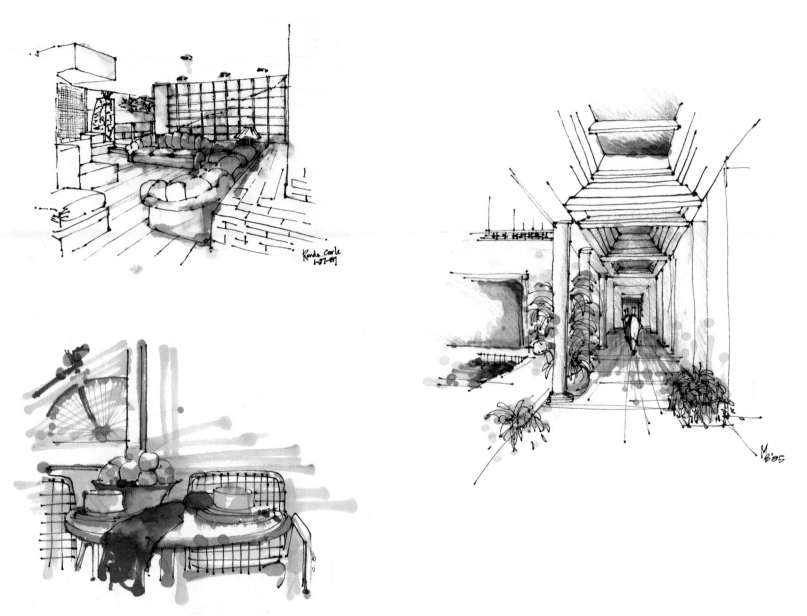

Figure 2-11. Participant, ML Graphic Workshop. Marker and felt-tip pen on 8″ × 8″ rice paper each. 30 minutes each.

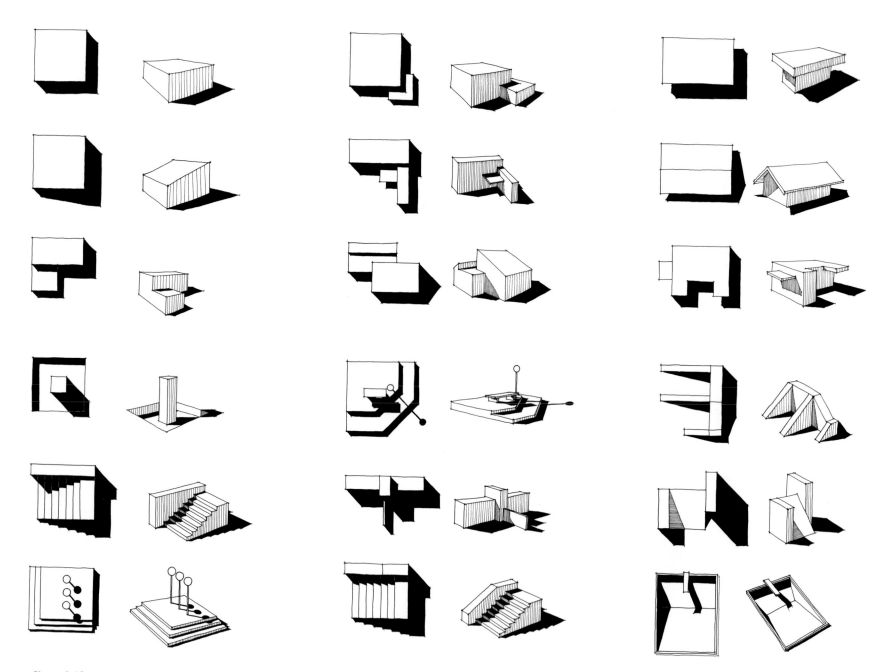

Figure 2-12. Participant, ML Graphic Workshop. Pen and ink on 19″ × 24″ layout paper. 12 hours.

3. 永 RENDERING TECHNIQUES

In order to generate a good rendering, one must be familiar with the techniques necessary to apply the proper medium. In this chapter, twenty rendering techniques will be explored. These techniques are categorized into three sections: "How to See" will enhance the reader's perception and understanding of how objects are represented; "How to Draw" will train the reader to draw with speed and confidence; and finally, "How to Apply" will explain the application of the techniques presented. Drawings of a doorknob will be used to illustrate some of these techniques. The twenty techniques that are discussed in this chapter are listed below:

TWENTY RENDERING TECHNIQUES

How to See
1. Two-Tone Contour Line
2. High Contrast
3. Ten-Tone Contour Line
4. Monotone
5. Monochromatic
6. Photo-Rendering Study
7. Collage

How to Draw
8. Continuous Line
9. Construction Line
10. Positive/Negative
11. Punch Line
12. Border Composition
13. Abstract Illustration

How to Apply
14. Tone Value
15. Line Value
16. Tone/Line Value Combined
17. Pointillism
18. Vertical/Horizontal Line
19. Cross-Hatching
20. Computer Application

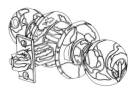

HOW TO SEE

1. Two-Tone Contour Line
This technique separates the values of an object into two tones. Light values (from 0 to 5) are grouped into one area labeled 0, and dark values (from 6 to 10) into another area labeled 10.

HOW: Using a color photograph of an object from a magazine, make a black-and-white copy and study its value changes. Separate the value changes into two groups with lines in between.

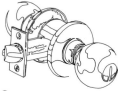

2. High Contrast
The high contrast technique uses black and white with no intermediate tones to create forms. All values are represented by either black or white space.

HOW: Analyze the object and separate its values into two tones: on a scale of 0 to 10—from white to black—values between 0 and 5 are left white, and those between 6 and 10 become black.

This technique can often produce outstanding results, particularly for graphic art or logo illustrations. It requires the artist to make keen observations of an object and to exaggerate its value changes. It also teaches how to see these values and then reproduce them with the highest degree of contrast, in black and white.

3. Ten-Tone Contour Line
Ten different values are identified on an object, and a closed contour line is placed around each area.

HOW: Label each area with a number to represent its value. Assign 0 to white and 10 to black areas. The values in between range from lightest to darkest.

4. Monotone
The monotone technique requires a marker of only one value of a color. By applying several coats with the same marker, a variety of darker values can be achieved. The darker the value desired, the greater the number of coats which must be applied. This technique allows an artist to work with a minimal color palette.

HOW: Using a single light-valued marker, begin to color the areas as numbered according to the ten-tone contour line technique. Areas labeled 0 should be left white. Areas marked 1 will receive one coat of the marker; those numbered 2 receive two coats of the same marker, and so on. Allow at least 4 minutes of drying time before applying the next coat. Occasionally you can use a colorless blender marker to lighten the color; this will extend the range of value that can be produced with one marker.

5. Monochromatic
In the monochromatic technique, a single color and all its values are used to finish a rendering. This is more effective than the monotone technique because it produces greater value contrast.

HOW: Using the ten-tone contour line as a base, apply gray markers ranging in value from 1 to 9, plus black. Leave 0 areas white and areas numbered 10 become black. This technique is extremely beneficial to the beginner, because with a limited color choice the beginner avoids many of the mistakes made in multicolored drawings.

6. Photo-Rendering Study
The photo-rendering approach is designed

to train the artist to see value changes and to record these in a rendering. You will need a photograph or reproduction.

HOW: Cut a photograph or reproduction in two. Keep one side of the image and reproduce the other side in a black and white or color rendering. Finally, splice the two together to complete the image. A more developed version of this technique is particularly useful to the professional who can use renderings of proposed structures and insert them into photographs of the existing environment. In this way the client can see the visual impact of proposed buildings.

7. Collage
In general there are two types of collage. One consists of little pieces of paper of different colors, tones, and values that are glued closely together to form the desired image. The other is a photo montage in which entire forms (trees, figures, cars, and so on) are cut out and positioned. These techniques represent substantial investments in time, with minimal costs. Collage is best for art work rather than presentation drawings for the client. It is extremely helpful in recognizing the many subtle changes in color and value that exist in any given form.

HOW: On an outlined sketch or drawing, apply adhesive to a small area. Select desired colors and values from pictures in a magazine. Cut or tear the pictures into small pieces and apply them to the sketch. Use the

edge of the picture as the outline of the object in your sketch.

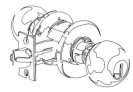

HOW TO DRAW
8. Continuous Line
Continuous line represents perhaps one of the most important developmental exercises in strengthening one's drawing skills. It enhances one's ability to draw confidently, boldly, and loosely, and it stimulates the right side of the brain.

HOW: Select a subject and draw it as quickly as possible, rarely lifting the pen or pencil from the paper. Focus more on the object being drawn than the drawing being made, concentrate more on proportion than on detail. The continuous line technique is seldom used for final presentation graphics but is highly recommended as an exercise.

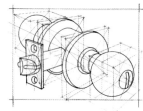

9. Construction Line
Construction line technique is used to explore and reveal the structure of a form. This technique is a quick way to sketch or plot a schematic design. It is often used as an approach to a more elaborate final drawing.

HOW: Use a light pencil line and sketch the basic forms and proportions of the object. With construction line drawing techniques, no value is delineated, and details are rarely shown. Construction lines may be applied with a pencil or colored pencil.

10. Positive/Negative

The positive/negative technique, like the continuous line technique, teaches the artist to see and reproduce objects clearly. It forces the artist to visualize design elements as a whole, not in parts, by reducing the drawing to positive space (the object) and negative space (the page or background). Details are eliminated and the artist is then able to concentrate exclusively on the form and its proportion.

HOW: Draw the object in silhouette. One line is used to identify both positive and negative space. This technique can be used to delineate complicated elements such as the tree foliage, chairs, etc.

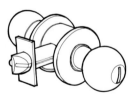

11. Punch Line

The punch line is also known as the profile line. It is a series of line weights used to accentuate targeted forms. Punch lines add emphasis to elements in the drawing and bring them forward. They differentiate the various elements and give the appearance of depth. This technique is suitable for quick sketches in pencil or felt-tip pen or for high-quality drawing in pen and ink.

HOW: On a sketch, the heaviest line weight is used to separate and define objects from sky. Medium line weight is used to separate objects from each other, and the thinnest line weight is used to show the portion of the object closest to the foreground.

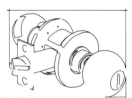

12. Border Composition

This technique focusses on the outline of forms within the drawing and their relationship to each other and to the edge of the page. No values are represented; instead, line (usually a closed contour line) is used to draw the subject and to bleed the outermost edges of the object off the edge of the page. This technique can enhance a line drawing and turn an otherwise marginal work into a successful rendering.

HOW: On a sketch, connect lines on the outside edge of the objects to form a border and create zig-zag or uneven edges. Several attempts may be needed to ensure a good result.

13. Abstract Illustration

Abstract illustration is used in graphic arts but never as a presentation drawing. Closely related to the contour line technique, abstraction combines closed contours with areas of solid color.

HOW: Using a closed contour line, isolate up to ten values in the subject, from white (0) to black (10). Assign each number a color and use these colors to fill in the corresponding area. Color selection for any given element within the drawing is flexible but should be reasonably appropriate for identification: sky and water being shades of blue, for example, and trees a combination of greens. This form of rendering can produce very visually exciting results. It is most appropriate for advertising and graphic illustration work, and forces the artist to represent values, forms, and space in a manner to which he is not usually accustomed.

HOW TO APPLY

14. Tone Value

Tone value technique uses value instead of line to delineate forms. It is considered to be the most lifelike technique, representing things as we actually see them. It is based on a solid understanding of light and its characteristics, including shade and shadow. Tone value drawings are usually highly prized as a final presentation graphic for the client.

HOW: Very lightly sketch the outlines of your subject. These should not be visible in the finished drawing. Using pastel, watercolor, or tempera, render the drawing from light to dark. You can also use airbrush, but expect to take more time than with other media.

15. Line Value

Line value drawings are renderings in line. It is used extensively by the architectural professions as it is fast and can make the product extremely appealing to clients. It is especially recommended for preliminary presentations and quick studies, although in a refined form it is very suitable for final graphics.

HOW: Line value drawings may be done in pencil, pen, and marker. A relatively thin line is usually recommended to achieve the best results, although often a combination of different line weights may be best. Study and use the principles of graphics that apply to line (see chap. 2).

16. Tone/Line Value Combined

Combining tone and line value drawings offers the greatest flexibility and is preferred by many professionals. It incorporates the best qualities of each and can be used with a variety of techniques.

HOW: A drawing can be done with marker or watercolor to achieve tone, and pencil, colored pencil, and pen and ink can then be used to finish the details. Choice of medium is determined by the intended use of the graphic, the skill level of the artist, and the time required to reach a finished product.

17. Pointillism

Pointillism, or "stippling," means rendering value changes with dots. This technique, though somewhat time consuming, can give the drawing a very soft and refined appearance. It is most appropriate for black-and-white reproduction, although by using colored inks or pens a colored drawing can be produced.

HOW: Select an appropriate size dot relative to the scale of the drawing, and apply the dots repeatedly to the drawing. As a general rule, smaller dots will produce a better quality rendering. Apply more dots to darker areas and fewer dots to lighter areas.

18. Vertical/Horizontal Line

Vertical and horizontal line techniques create form and value with parallel lines. As in pointillism, shapes are identified through value changes rather than outline. Both vertical and horizontal line techniques, which use pen and ink most often, are very time consuming, but allow for interesting results, particularly when viewed from a distance.

HOW: Select appropriate line weights, and using only vertical or horizontal lines, apply them to the drawing. The closer the lines are to one another, the darker the value created. Use only one line weight at a time, throughout the entire drawing.

19. Cross-Hatching

Cross-hatching uses crossed lines to identify value changes and forms. Pencil or pen and ink are the most appropriate mediums. While cross-hatching is extremely time consuming, it can result in a superb final presentation drawing.

HOW: This technique, like pointillism and vertical/horizontal line techniques, relies upon the density of pattern to establish value: the closer the pattern of lines, the darker the value. Lines making up the cross-hatching pattern may be placed at any angle to each other, although the direction should reinforce the shape of the object which is being depicted. Line weight may vary within the cross-hatching, but thin lines are usually best.

20. Computer Application

Computer graphics has become very popular in recent years. Although it takes time to master, the results can be very impressive.

Computer application in graphics has both advantages and disadvantages. The advantages include allowing artists to manipulate their work without fear of ruining the original, to print graphics with smooth, crisp lines and edges, and to experiment with color quickly and easily. CADD programs allow one to view the space in three dimensions and to see the design in a walk-through sequence of the spaces. Once all possible views are examined, one may choose the angle most suitable to the final rendering. The disadvantage of the computer is that the artist is almost automatically put into the left-side mode of the brain, and working on a two-dimensional computer screen can inhibit creativity and the looseness needed for impulsive, imaginative renderings. However, the computer is an important and useful tool, especially for some of the time-consuming tasks. Its use should be combined with personal creativity and application of the principles presented in this book.

HOW: There are many types of software programs and explanatory literature available on the market. Review the various programs and their capabilities. When you find the program best suited to your needs, use it to create the desired framework of a sketch and render it accordingly.

EXAMPLES: See figures 3-1 to 3-6 for some example of rendering techniques.

Figure 3-1. Participants, ML Graphic Workshop. Felt-tip pen on 9″ × 12″ sketch paper each. 3 to 25 minutes each.

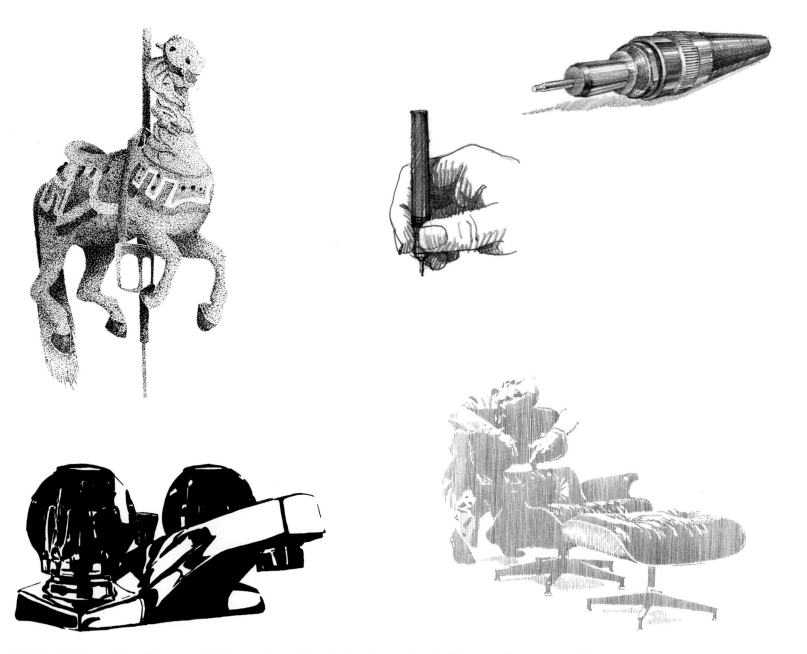

Figure 3-2. Top left: Christine Hess, Washington, DC. Pen and ink on 8½″ × 11″ vellum. 2 hours. Top right: Dick Sneary, Kansas City, MO. Pencil on 8″ × 10″ sketch paper. 1 hour. Bottom left, bottom right: participants, ML Graphic Workshop. Pen and ink on 6″ × 8″ sketch paper each. 30 minutes to 1 hour each.

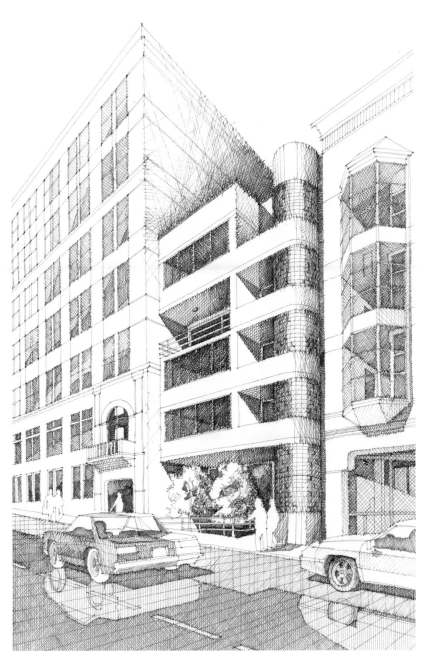

Figure 3-3. Left: Craig Patterson & Associates, Kansas City, MO. Felt-tip pen on 8½" × 11" white tracing paper each. 1 hour each. Right: John Yancey, participant, ML Graphic Workshop. Pen and ink on 14" × 20" vellum. 5 hours.

UNIT A   FAMILY·ROTUNDA

unit c

BROOKINGS   10.29.89   RIDGLEY HALL   10.29.89   Figure 3-4

Figure 3-4. Top: Chad Moor, Bloodgood Architects, Inc., Des Moines, IA. Pen and ink on 12″ × 14″ mylar each. 2 to 4 hours each. Bottom left: Craig Roberts, for Edward D. Stone, Jr. and Associates, Fort Lauderdale, FL. Marker and felt-tip pen on 24″ × 36″ rice paper. 10 hours. Bottom right: Rod Henmi, Washington University. Pen and ink on 5″ × 8″ sketch paper each. 30 minutes each.

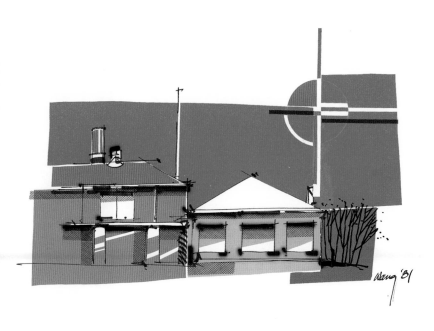

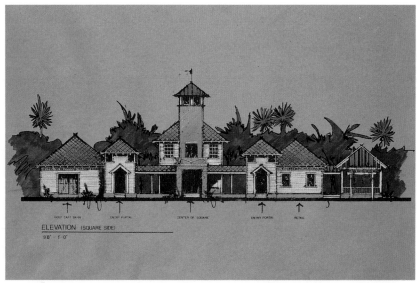

Figure 3-5. Top left: Karl Amsler. Paper collage (magazine fragments) on 8½″ × 11″ Xerox paper. 12 hours. Top right: Thomas Wang, Watertown, MA. Felt-tip pen and colored Pantone on 10″ × 12″ bristol paper. 45 minutes. Bottom left: Craig Patterson & Associates, Kansas City, MO. Colored pencil on 16″ × 20″ Letraset Pantone colored paper (original, color photograph). 32 hours. Bottom right: Deborah Wood, Edward D. Stone, Jr. and Associates, Fort Lauderdale, FL. Marker, colored pencil, and pastel on 24″ × 36″ kraft paper. 4 hours.

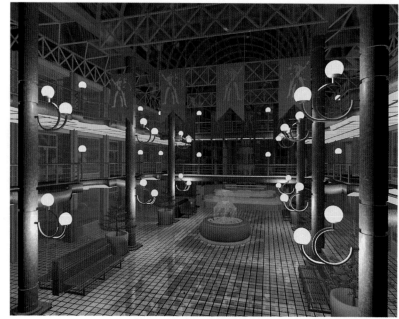

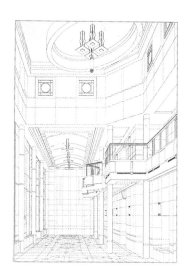

Figure 3-6. Top left: Gen Obata and Dave van Bakergem, Urban Research and Design Center, Washington University, St. Louis, MO. Produced on an IOLINE LP3700 pen plotter on 10″ × 20″ computer paper. Top right: Point Line Graphics, Inc., Middleton, WI. POINT LINE CADD on 6″ × 10″ computer paper. Bottom: David Nobles, Howard Needles Tammen & Bergendoff, Kansas City, MO. Airbrush on 20″ × 30″ watercolor paper each (original with CADD). 80 hours (including CADD and rendering time.)

4. 永 RENDERING TYPES

Generally, all renderings or illustrations can be accomplished by using one of the three types of medium: dry, semiwet, and wet.

Dry media are non-water-soluble, usually eradicable, easily portable, and quick to apply. Dry media also readily produce the gradual value change essential to most drawings.

Semiwet media include ink and marker, which although wet when applied, are considered semiwet because they dry very quickly. Semiwet media can be used to produce either tone or line for gradual value changes within a drawing. The variety of color selection, combined with the ease of application, make them ideal for professionals and beginners.

Wet media require water for application and are water soluble, as in the case of watercolor, tempera, and gouache. They are generally noneradicable. Normally the greatest amount of skill is required to use them successfully; different pigments must be blended together to produce subtle value changes. Wet medium techniques, however, allow the artist to cover large areas quickly and provide the greatest possible range of colors available.

Along with the three basic media types, there are mixed media techniques which are often used to create special effects. This may include wet media with wet, wet with dry, or dry with dry media. Mixed media can be especially useful in making changes or corrections. An opaque medium, such as tempera, will easily cover a transparent medium such as marker, for example, masking errors. The twenty-seven rendering types

in which eight are discussed in depth in the next section are listed below.

TWENTY-SEVEN RENDERING TYPES
Dry Media (Pencil and Pastel)
1. Regular Pencil
2. Carpenter Pencil
3. Black Colored Pencil
4. Charcoal Pencil
5. Colored Pencil
6. Colored Pencil on Black or Brown Line Print Paper

7. Regular Pastel
8. Pastel on Yellow Tracing Paper

Semiwet Media (Ink and Marker)
9. Regular Ink
10. Ink Wash
11. Colored Zip with Ink Outlined
12. Black and White Zip with Ink Outlined

13. Regular Marker
14. Marker with Colored Pencil
15. Marker with Ink Acetate Overlay
16. Marker with Tempera and Pastel
17. Marker on Yellow Tracing Paper
18. Marker on Print Paper (Charcoal Original)
19. Marker on Mylar
20. Marker on Sepia Print Paper

Wet Media (Watercolor, Tempera, Airbrush, and Acrylics)
21. Regular Watercolor
22. Watercolor with Ink Outlined
23. Watercolor and Tempera Mixed

24. Regular Tempera

25. Regular Airbrush
26. Airbrush with Ink Outlined on Sepia Paper

27. Acrylic with Ink Outlined

Of these rendering types eight are most

commonly used by professionals: pencil, colored pencil, pastel, pen and ink, marker, watercolor, tempera, and airbrush. Each one is detailed below. A complete understanding of the medium and a wise choice of media can determine the success of your project. Before you begin, review the principles outlined in chapter 2 and, for each medium, choose materials appropriate to your goals.

For each medium there is a short introduction that acquaints the reader with the rendering type, its overall characteristics, capabilities, limitations, and appropriate use. The most commonly used art materials are then listed. Simple step-by-step procedures that illustrate the best approaches to the medium follow. There is a list of technical tips to help you get the most out of the medium. Illustrations explain the techniques. And finally, there are examples, or sample drawings, that incorporate the principles of good graphics.

PENCIL

Pencil renderings may be classified into two groups: graphite and wax-based pencils. Because the pencil is versatile and can produce value through solid tone or line, it is a favorite among many professionals. Pencil renderings, especially graphite-based ones, are easily erased, allowing for instant alterations. One type of lead can produce many values within a drawing. Pencil types include graphite, charcoal, Prismacolor black pencil, and China marker and other wax-based pencils. Although sometimes used to produce finished renderings, the pencil's most appropriate use is for the quick sketch.

Materials
Pencils with the following numbers and designations: No. 2, HB, 2B, 6B; KOH-

I-NOOR "Negro" No. 2; Wolff's Carbon BB, Eagle 314; Dixon No. 303; 6B Carpenter Pencil.

Step-by-Step

1. Chisel the point and rough in the basic forms of the drawing. Make sure you are satisfied with the perspective and the composition (fig. 4-1).

2. Trace desired outlines on an appropriate paper and determine value and white space required, noticing shade and shadow areas.

3. Layout the composition, using wrist and arm instead of hand movements, applying 45-degree strokes with a gradual value change. Work from one side of the page or object to the other, and from light to dark areas to avoid smudging.

4. Add details, shade, and shadow. Once the rendering is completed, spray with fixative to adhere pencil to the paper. Use a workable fixative to allow for later changes and corrections to the original.

Technical Tips

• Keep eraser use to a minimum.
• Use direction of stroke to reinforce the contours of the surface you are depicting.
• Start pencil strokes along the edge of a sheet of paper or stop strokes with the edge of a triangle or straightedge to give the illusion of an outline (fig. 4-2).
• Create special textures by placing a coarse, textured material under the drawing, and then applying the pencil.
• Create highlighted areas such as a cloud in the sky or a water feature by erasing with a kneaded eraser or an electric eraser.

EXAMPLES: See figures 4-3 and 4-4 for sample drawings that incorporate the principles discussed.

1. Rough out perspective sketch.

2. Trace desired outlines onto an appropriate paper.

3. Layout the composition.

4. Add details, shade, and shadow.

Figure 4-1.

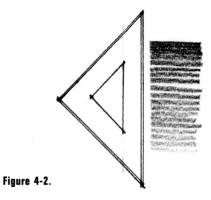

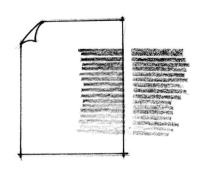

Figure 4-2.

Figure 4-3. Bottom left: Robert Boulton, St Louis, MO. Pencil on 8½" × 11" white tracing paper. 1 hour and 30 minutes. Top right: Gary Mellenbruch, Kansas City, MO. Pencil on 12" × 16" sketch paper. 2 hours.

Figure 4-4. Jim Hayes, illustrator, for Belt, Collins and Associates, Honolulu, HI. Carbon pencil on 14″×20″ vellum. 10 hours.

COLORED PENCIL

Colored pencils can add excitement to a rendering. They blend easily, control well, and can create light or value changes quickly. As a medium, colored pencil is extremely appealing for a presentation.

Available in as many as 120 colors, colored pencils, which are wax based, do not reflect light the way graphite pencils do. They resist moisture and fading. They can be used on a variety of grounds—different boards and papers—which can produce a multitude of textures. Colored-pencil rendering may be made without outline, and if well applied, may result in extremely realistic effects.

Colored pencils are "user-friendly" and are as effective for quick design studies as for final presentation graphics. However, because of their thin strokes, using them can be time-consuming.

Materials

Berol Prismacolor pencil sets of 48 or 60, or put together the following colors: white, warm gray 20%, warm gray 50%, black; blush pink, carmine red, scarlet lake, crimson red, orange; cream, canary yellow, yellow ochre, raw umber, sepia, peach; green bice, apple green, olive green, grass green, true green; light cerulean blue, true blue, copenhagen blue, indigo blue, aquamarine.

Step-by-Step

1. Use a red colored pencil to rough in a sketch on paper (fig.4-5).
2. Apply light base colors. Work from one side of the page to the other. Chisel the point on each colored pencil you use and apply color from light to dark. Leave appropriate white space.

1. Rough out sketch using a red pencil.

2. Apply base colors.

3. Add more as well as darker colors.

Figure 4-5.

4. Outline with a black colored pencil and add details.

3. Add more as well as darker colors. Do not forget color principles (chapter 2).
4. Finally, outline with a black colored pencil and use it to tone down the value if necessary. Add details as needed.

When the drawing has been completed, use a fixative to preserve it and to prevent smudging.

Technical Tips

• Study the technical tips given for pencil rendering.

• Start with the lightest color and gradually add darker values.

• Use smooth-textured paper to achieve a crisp and more realistic drawing.

• Do not "paint by numbers." When you use a color, repeat it on every object in the drawing, but provide more green in the trees, more brown on the trunk, more blue in the sky, and so on.

• Use color pair to excite the drawing; for example, add red to the grass, orange to the sky, or a yellow cushion to a purple chair.

• Apply earthy tone colors. Avoid the use of bright colors, if possible, to achieve the most realistic effects.

• Outline and add details with a black colored pencil.

• Use the black colored pencil to wash over areas and tone values down, creating a well-balanced color effect. This is usually done after all the colors have been applied.

EXAMPLES: See figures 4-6 to 4-7 for sample drawings that incorporate the principles discussed.

Figure 4-6. Scott Arbogast, participant, ML Graphic Workshop. Colored pencil on 10″ × 16″ yellow tracing paper each. 1 to 2 hours each.

W E S T *looking West* E N D

Figure 4-7. Michael Doyle, Boulder, CO. Colored pencil on 8½″ × 11″ photocopy paper (original, pen and ink on vellum). 8 hours.

PASTEL

Pastel rendering is extremely effective for fast sketches. Pastel is often used to cover large areas quickly. The wide range of colors allows you to select appropriately for an entire rendering or for highlights in other media. Chalky in composition, pastels are often overlooked because they are somewhat messy. However, they can be added to a line drawing to produce a good colored rendering with an almost watercolor-like appearance. Pastels are highly recommended for rendering skies, lakes, and other bodies of water, and any large area that needs subtle value changes and fine texture.

Materials

Eberhard Faber Nupastel; Grumbacher Golden palette pastels; 12 or 24 square sticks.

Step-by-Step

1. With a red or regular pencil, lightly rough in a sketch on paper (fig. 4-8).
2. Apply the desired base pastel colors to the drawing. Work from lightest to darkest value areas and from one side of the drawing to the other to avoid smudging.
3. Add more as well as darker colors, applying workable fixative to areas as you complete them to prevent smudges. Once all the pastel has been applied, fix the entire drawing with the workable fixative.
4. Use black colored pencils to outline the entire drawing and other colored pencils to add fine details that cannot be made with pastel. Finally, apply clear plastic fixative to the entire drawing to preserve it.

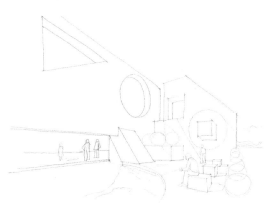

1. Rough in a sketch and outline with a red pencil.

2. Apply desired pastel color.

3. Add more as well as darker colors.

Figure 4-8.

4. Outline with black colored pencil and add details.

Technical Tips

• Break the pastel stick to a workable size. Lightly apply its entire corner edge to the paper. Avoid making a hard line (fig. 4-9).

• If a fine texture is desired, such as in skies, water, or grass, use your fingertips or a blending stick to create surface and value changes.

• Always start to work at one edge of the object being delineated, stopping the stroke at the other edge with different pressure to create gradual value change (fig. 4-10).

• Follow color principles (see chapter 2). Once a color is used, it needs to be repeated on every object or area in the drawing.

• Rough textured paper may be placed under the rendering to achieve a variety of textures in the drawing. Simply apply pastel over the original drawing and the texture will show through.

EXAMPLES: See figures 4-11 and 4-12 for sample drawings that incorporate the techniques discussed.

Figure 4-9.

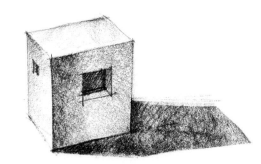

Figure 4-10.

Figure 4-11. Dick Sneary, Kansas City, MO. Pastel on 20″ × 30″ white tracing paper. 1 hour.

Figure 4-12. Dick Sneary, Kansas City, MO. Pastel on 18″ × 24″ yellow tracing paper. 5 hours.

Pen and Ink

Pen-and-ink is probably the most widely used black and white technique by design professionals. Application methods range from felt-tip pens to technical pens. The medium may be used with either freehand or mechanical approaches. Its opaque characteristics make it ideal for black-and-white reproductions and prints. Ink techniques are noneradicable and require combinations of line tones to establish textures and value changes: dots, vertical or horizontal lines, cross-hatching, and doodling patterns are all used for this purpose.

Pen-and-ink can easily be combined with other media. It is most frequently used as a base to which color is added. Colored pencil, marker, watercolor, acrylic, and airbrush are all used. Value changes represented by ink techniques alone are usually not realistic and demand a combined media approach for optimum effects.

Materials
Rapidograph pen set (000-4); Sharpie by Sanford; felt-tip pens by Flair, Pilot, Shaeffer, and LePen.

Step-by-Step
1. Use pencil to rough a perspective sketch on paper (fig. 4-13).
2. Add elements and adjust composition.
3. Trace desired outlines on a drawing paper with pen and ink.
4. Add details, shade, and shadow using the techniques described in chapter 3.

Technical Tips
• When outlining the rendering, use the thinnest lines possible.
• Vary line thicknesses to differentiate the depth within the drawing. Things close up

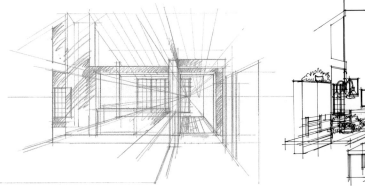

1. Rough in a perspective sketch.

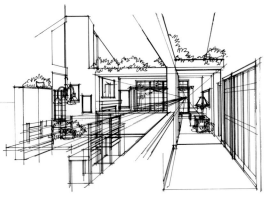

2. Add elements and adjust the composition.

3. Trace desired outlines onto a separate paper with pen and ink.

4. Add details, shade, and shadow.

Figure 4-13.

have a thick line; those far away have a thin line.
• Proper delineation of shade and shadow areas is extremely important to this technique.
• Generally, use of mechanical line is quicker, and freehand line will take more time since it needs to trace over the constructed mechanical line. However, the freehand line will give the drawing a more pleasant and loose appearance.

• Apply commercially made pounce to waxy vellum and mylar surfaces to prevent the pen from skipping.
• Try using a different colored ink in place of black. Brown ink gives the drawing a particularly soft and pleasant visual effect.

EXAMPLES: See figures 4-14 to 4-15 for drawings that incorporate the techniques discussed.

Figure 4-14. Left: Brian Swanson, Baltimore, MD. Pen and ink on 24" × 30" vellum. 24 hours. Top right: Chad Moor; bottom right: Sherman Shook, Bloodgood Architects, Inc., Des Moines, IA. Pen and ink on 12" × 18" mylar each. 4 to 6 hours each.

Figure 4-15. Left: Chad Moor; top right: Sherman Shook; bottom right: Shannon Gordon, Bloodgood Architects, Inc., Des Moines, IA. Pen and ink and felt-tip pen on 16″ × 24″ vellum each. 1 to 8 hours each.

1. Rough in a sketch using a red pencil.

2. Trace desired outlines and add details onto vellum with pen and ink.

3. Render the base color with marker on diazo print paper.

4. Add darker colors and details with colored pencils.

Figure 4-16.

MARKER

Marker, unlike any other medium, is applied wet but dries almost instantly. It is like watercolor applied with a penlike instrument. Realistic colors may be easily achieved without mixing colors or using a brush. This medium is very versatile. There is a wide color selection, a wide choice of nibs in applicators, and a compatibility with other media such as colored pencil.

Unlike other wet media, markers may be used on almost any type of paper, including vellum and tracing paper, to obtain different values and effects. The original may fade over time, however, particularly if it is exposed to direct sunlight over a prolonged period of time. This can be prevented by photographing or reproducing the original for display purposes.

Materials
Markers come in a wide variety of colors. See Appendix D.

Step-by-Step: General
1. Use a red or regular pencil first to rough in a sketch (fig. 4-16).
2. On vellum, trace desired outlines and add details with pencil or pen and ink.
3. On the diazo print paper, start with the lightest markers and concentrate on one subject at a time, adding a darker value gradually in order to achieve a good blending result and to prevent a water-mark appearance (fig. 4-17).
4. Complete the drawing by adding darker colors and details with colored pencils or other media.

Step-by-Step: Creating a Gradual Value Change
1. Select 3 to 5 markers from the same color range with values from light to dark (fig. 4-18).
2. Apply the lightest color vertically several times to the entire area (fig. 4-19).
3. While the lightest color is still wet, use the next darker color to cover approximately two-thirds of the area. Apply it toward the right edge of the area several times to maintain the wetness (fig. 4-20). Immediately use the first color and apply it vertically several times where the two colors meet until the line becomes less prominent (fig. 4-21
4. While the second color is still wet, use the next darker color to cover the remaining one-third of the area. Apply the marker toward the right edge (fig. 4-22). Immediately use the second color to clean the line between the two colors (fig. 4-23).
5. Repeat the process if more colors are used. Using a colorless blender as the lightest color will give the drawing a soft watercolor-like appearance.

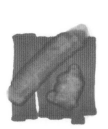

Figure 4-17.

Figure 4-18.

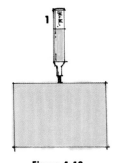

Figure 4-19.

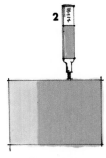

Figure 4-20.

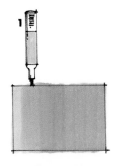

Figure 4-21.

Figure 4-22.

Figure 4-23.

Technical Tips

• When outlines of the original drawing are not readily visible, it is necessary to outline the entire drawing again with a black felt-tip pen. The lighter the value and the smaller the size of a drawing, the thinner the pen that should be used.

• Marker colors may be mixed by applying one color on top of another. For example, blue over yellow will result in green (fig. 4-24).

• To create stripes, apply the first coat of marker and wait 2 to 3 minutes for it to dry, then use the same marker to draw over the desired area (fig. 4-25).

• Applying two coats of a color, waiting between coats, will make the next darker value. For example, two coats of gray No. 4 will equal gray No. 5 (fig. 4-26).

• Create a marker chart with a wide spectrum selection and good range of values for quick reference.

• Markers dry easily in a hot, dry environment. They should be kept in a cool place. If a marker does become dry, it may be rejuvenated by adding a few drops of lighter fluid, rubber cement thinner, or Toluene. This will somewhat reduce the intensity of color.

• Never throw away old markers. Dry markers can often be used to make lighter values and special effects.

• Use index cards, masking tape, or other appropriate material as a frisket, or mask, for a smooth straight-lined look (fig. 4-27).

• Strokes made with a straightedge such as a triangle often leave a black smudge line. Using an inch-wide cardboard or chipboard strip as the straightedge can eliminate this problem; marker fluid will be absorbed into the board and will not pick up the previous lines.

• Blending a rough gradual value change can be achieved by using a white colored pencil. Apply the white colored pencil from one side to the other gradually reducing the pressure (fig. 4-28).

• Use a white colored pencil or Pelican graphic white ink to add highlights if necessary.

• In order to achieve a shiny appearance on flat surfaces, use vertical strokes of the same color of the object being reflected.

• To correct a mistake, use a darker color or an opaque medium such as tempera to cover it, or simply cut out the area, attach new paper, and redo that part of the drawing.

EXAMPLES: See figures 4-29 to 4-33 for sample drawings that incorporate the techniques discussed.

Figure 4-24.

Figure 4-25.

Figure 4-26.

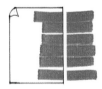

Figure 4-27.

Figure 4-28.

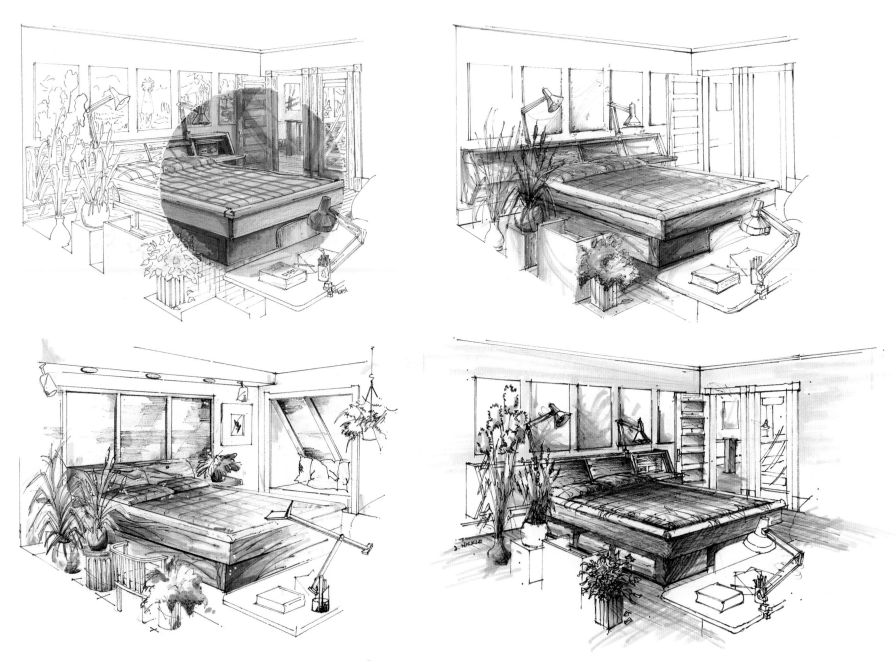

Figure 4-29. Top left: Stacey Karst; top right: Galiger; bottom left: Alicia Ching; bottom right: James Nickle, participants, ML Graphic Workshop. Marker, colored pencil, and felt-tip pen on 19″ × 24″ marker paper each. 1 to 2 hours each.

Figure 4-30. Top left: Thomas Wang, Watertown, MA. Marker on 10″ × 14″ marker paper. 30 minutes. Top right: Scott Collard; bottom: Scott Nesbitt, participants, ML Graphic Workshop. Marker, colored pencil, and felt-tip pen on 19″ × 24″ marker paper each. 1 to 2 hours each.

Figure 4-31. Craig Roberts, Edward D. Stone, Jr. and Associates, Fort Lauderdale, FL. Marker and felt-tip pen on 24″ × 36″ rice paper each. 8 to 12 hours each.

ENGLEWOOD DOWNTOWN
CIVIC CENTER BLVD. – LOOKING WEST

EDAW inc., Landscape Architects
McLaughlin Water Engineers

FRAGRANCE GARDEN
Denver Botanic Gardens

EDAW

Figure 4-32. Top: EDAW, Fort Collins, CO. Marker on 24″ × 36″ blackline diazo print paper tracing paper each. 20 hours each (original, pencil on mylar). Bottom left: Craig Roberts, Edward D. Stone, Jr. and Associates, Fort Lauderdale, FL. Marker on 36″ × 42″ blackline diazo print paper. (original, felt-tip pen on white tracing paper). 8 hours. Bottom right: Johnson, Johnson & Roy Inc, Ann Arbor, MI. Marker on 8″ × 12″ sepia paper (original, pencil on tracing paper). 3 hours.

Figure 4-54. Top left: Shannon Gordon, participant, ML Graphic Workshop. Marker and felt-tip pen on 10″ × 15″ marker paper. 30 minutes. Top right: Robert Hanna, Lincoln, NE. Watercolor on 10″ × 15″ watercolor paper. 1 hour. Bottom left: Gary Mellenbruch, Kansas City, MO. Tempera on 10″ × 15″ illustration board. 2 hours. Bottom right: Carolyn Caple, Participant, ML Graphic Workshop. Airbrush on 10″ × 15″ layout paper. 3 hours.

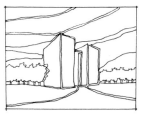
1. Two-Tone Contour Line

5. Monochromatic

9. Construction Line

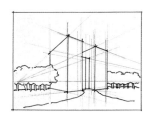
13. Abstract Illustration

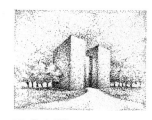
17. Pointillism

1. Regular Pencil

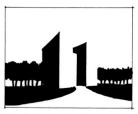
2. High Contrast

6. Photo-Rendering Study

10. Positive-Negative

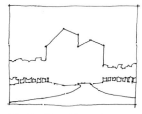
14. Tone Value

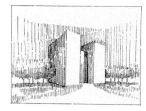
18. Vertical/Horizontal Line

2. Carpenter Pencil

3. Ten-Tone Contour Line

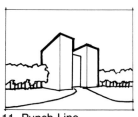
7. Collage

11. Punch Line

15. Line Value

19. Cross-Hatching

3. Black Colored P

4. Monotone

8. Continuous Line

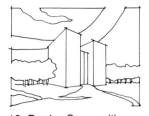
12. Border Composition

16. Tone/Line Value
Combined

20. Computer Application

4. Charcoal Pencil

Figure 4-54. The building study.

TWENTY-SEVEN RENDERING TYPES

Colored Pencil

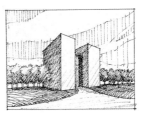

9. Regular Ink

13. Regular Marker

17. Marker on Yellow Tracing Paper

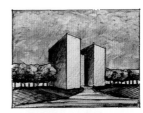

21. Regular Watercolor

25. Regular Airbrush

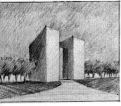

Colored Pencil on Black or Brown Line

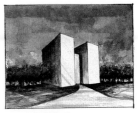

10. Ink Wash

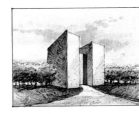

14. Marker with Colored Pencil

18. Marker on Print Paper (Charcoal Original)

22. Watercolor with Ink Outlined

26. Airbrush with Ink Outlined on Sepia

Regular Pastel

11. Colored Zip with Ink Outlined

15. Marker with Ink Acetate Overlay

19. Marker on Mylar

23. Watercolor and Tempera Mixed

27. Acrylic with Ink Outlined

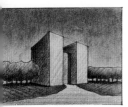

Pastel on Yellow Tracing Paper

12. Black and White Zip with Ink Outlined

16. Marker with Tempera and Pastel

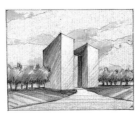

20. Marker on Sepia Print Paper

24. Regular Tempera

Rendered by the class of January 1992, Mike Lin Graphic Workshop.

Credit

MATRIX CHART

RENDERING TYPES

Dry Media (Pencil and Pastel)
1. Regular Pencil
2. Carpenter Pencil
3. Black Colored Pencil
4. Charcoal Pencil
5. Colored Pencil
6. Colored Pencil on Black or Brown Line
7. Regular Pastel
8. Pastel on Yellow Tracing Paper

Semiwet Media (Ink and Marker)
9. Regular Ink
10. Ink Wash
11. Colored Zip with Ink Outlined
12. Black and White Zip with Ink Outlined
13. Regular Marker
14. Marker with Colored Pencil
15. Marker with Ink Acetate Overlay
16. Marker with Tempera and Pastel
17. Marker on Yellow Tracing Paper
18. Marker on Print Paper (Charcoal Original)
19. Marker on Mylar
20. Marker on Sepia Print Paper

Wet Media (Watercolor, Tempera, Airbrush, and Acrylics)
21. Regular Watercolor
22. Watercolor with Ink Outlined
23. Watercolor and Tempera Mixed
24. Regular Tempera
25. Regular Airbrush
26. Airbrush with Ink Outlined on Sepia Paper
27. Acrylic with Ink Outlined

RENDERING TECHNIQUES

Technique	1	2	3	4	5	6	7	8	9	10	11	12	13	14	15	16	17	18	19	20	21	22	23	24	25	26	27	Time Req.	Client Sat.	Skill	Value
How to See																															
1. Two-Tone Contour Line	•	•	•	•					•																			1	1	1	1
2. High Contrast	•	•	•	•		•	•		•	•		•	•					•					•		•	•		1	2	1	2
3. Ten-Tone Contour Line	•	•	•	•					•																			2	1	2	1
4. Monotone													•															2	2	2	2
5. Monochromatic	•	•	•	•	•		•	•			•	•	•	•							•	•	•	•		•	•	3	3	3	4
6. Photo-Rendering Study	•	•	•	•	•	•	•	•		•			•			•		•			•	•	•	•	•	•	•	5	5	5	5
7. Collage																												5	1	3	1
How to Draw																															
8. Continuous Line	•	•	•	•	•				•				•															1	2	2	2
9. Construction Line	•	•	•	•	•		•		•																			2	2	2	2
10. Positive-Negative	•	•	•	•	•	•	•		•																			1	1	1	1
11. Punch Line	•	•	•	•	•	•	•		•				•															1	2	1	2
12. Border Composition	•	•	•	•	•	•	•						•					•										2	2	3	2
13. Abstract Illustration	•	•	•	•	•	•	•		•		•		•					•			•	•	•	•	•	•	•	2	1	2	1
How to Apply																															
14. Tone Value	•	•	•	•	•					•	•	•	•	•	•	•	•	•	•	•	•	•	•	•	•	•	•	4	5	5	5
15. Line Value	•	•	•	•	•	•			•																			4	4	5	4
16. Tone/Line Value Combined	•	•	•	•	•	•					•	•	•	•	•	•	•	•	•	•			•			•	•	5	5	5	5
17. Pointillism	•	•	•	•	•	•	•		•			•				•			•	•								5	3	3	4
18. Vertical/Horizontal Line	•	•	•	•	•				•							•			•	•								4	3	3	2
19. Cross-Hatching	•	•	•	•	•	•			•																			5	4	5	4
20. Computer Application																												5	5	5	4
Time Requirements	3	3	2	3	3	5	4	2	5	4	3	3	3	4	4	5	3	4	2	4	3	4	5	5	5	5	5				
Client Satisfaction	3	3	3	3	3	4	4	4	4	4	3	2	4	4	4	5	5	3	5	2	5	5	5	5	5	5	5				
Skill Level	3	3	3	3	3	4	4	4	4	4	3	2	2	4	4	4	5	5	4	5	5	5	5	5	5	5	5				
Value of Illustration	3	3	3	3	5	4	4	3	4	4	3	2	4	5	4	5	3	5	2	4	5	5	5	5	5	5	5				

Time Requirements	1=Least Time Spent	5=Most Time Spent
Client Satisfaction	1=Least Satisfied	5=Most Satisfied
Skill Level	1=Least Skill Required	5=Most Skill Required
Value of Illustration	1=Least Expensive	5=Most Expensive

5. 永 LETTERING

Lettering is integral to the overall composition of design projects. It is often used in plan, elevation, section, sketch, and perspective drawings. If not done properly, it can greatly affect the quality of a drawing.

In general, pencil lettering is appropriate for formal and detail drawings, while marker lettering is more suitable for quick preliminaries and presentation graphics. The step-by-step procedures below will help you to improve your lettering skills.

PENCIL LETTERING

For consistency, choose a universal lettering style instead of a highly individual one. Lettering shape should be kept square and not too elongated. Generally, letters should be no more than ½ inch high. If bigger lettering is required, a block letter style is recommended for good proportion (fig. 5-1).

Step-by-Step

1. Draw an even number of guidelines with a No. 2H, H, or F lead pencil. Or, if three guidelines are used, offset the middle line (fig. 5-2).

2. Chisel the point, and use hit-go-hit line with same thickness on all strokes, but do not overlap corners (fig. 5-3).

3. Use the broad edge of the chisel point to draw the horizontal line. Twist the pencil or wrist and use the narrow edge to draw the vertical line (fig. 5-4).

4. Draw all vertical lines with a straightedge; all horizontal, curved, and slanted lines freehand. Horizontal lines may be slanted upward slightly to create interest, but should always be kept parallel to each other (fig. 5-5).

5. Letters are spaced based upon area between each other, not distance. Practice lettering mostly in capitals, since they are used most frequently (fig. 5-6). Figure 5-7 is another example.

Figure 5-1.

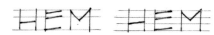

Figure 5-2.

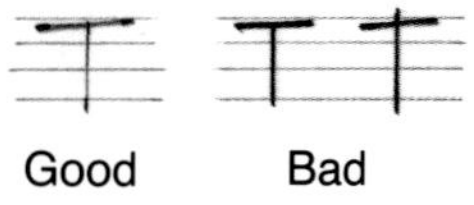

Good   Bad

Figure 5-3.

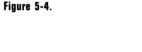

Figure 5-4.

Figure 5-5.

Good   Bad

Figure 5-6.

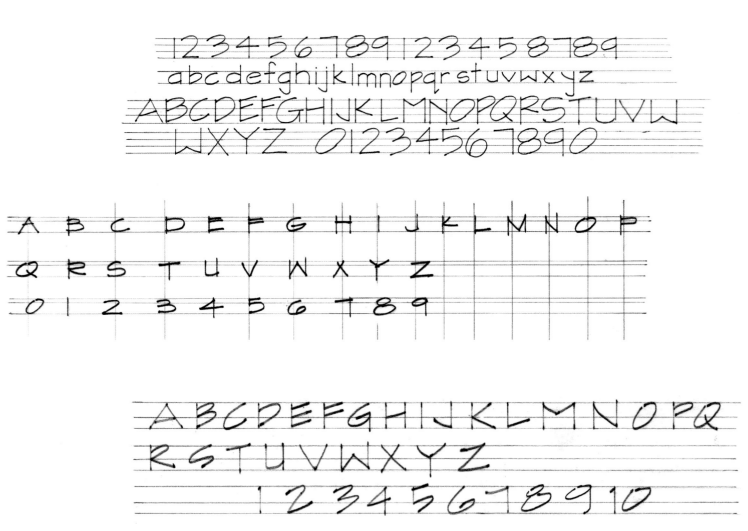

Figure 5-7. Top: Michael Doyle, Boulder, CO. Pen and ink on 1″ × 8″ bond paper. 5 minutes. Center, bottom: participant, ML Graphic Workshop. Pencil on 8½″ × 11″ bond paper. 30 minutes.

MARKER LETTERING

Marker lettering is accomplished in much the same way that pencil lettering is. The thickness of the marker stroke is based on size of the lettering. Bigger letters will require thicker strokes. Do not overlap corners of marker strokes and keep the overall shape of the letter square (fig. 5-8).

Step-by-Step

1. Construct guidelines in pencil.

2. Use a broad-tip marker to draw desired letters; use of a straightedge is encouraged (fig. 5-9).

3. With the 3-D line technique, use a Sharpie pen to outline a letter drawn with marker, leaving no white space. Outline again with a thin felt-tip pen, leaving a small gap between lines. Use hit-go-hit, overlap corner, professional dots, and professional gaps when outlining (fig. 5-10).

4. Letters may be further highlighted by adding stripes with a second coat of the same marker. Apply pastel or colored pencil (fig. 5-11).

5. Block letters can be created by tracing from commercial press-on letter sheets; this is more economical than using actual press-type. Or use a colorless blender or very light marker and draw the letters on paper. Outline the letter immediately with pen or pencil, while the marker fluid is still wet. See figure 5-12 for marker lettering example.

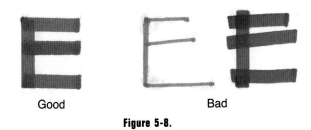

Good   Bad

Figure 5-8.

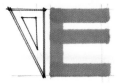

Figure 5-9.

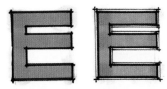

Figure 5-10.   **Figure 5-11.**

Figure 5-12. Participants, ML Graphic Workshop. Marker, colored pencil, and felt-tip pen on 19″ × 24″ marker paper. 10 minutes to 1 hour each.

6. 永 ENTOURAGE

The addition of entourage and miscellaneous elements helps create a lifelike appearance and enriches the composition of the drawing. Undesirable elements may be hidden, while interesting points can be emphasized.

Entourage consists of the elements in the drawing that accompany and enhance the focal point—everything from sky and trees to cars and people. It adds scale to the drawing and presents the design more clearly. Overall, entourage makes the drawing more believable and understandable. For example, a building rendered without people or trees loses its sense of scale and is not as enticing as one that includes interesting entourage.

PEOPLE

People in a drawing provide that all-important human element. They suggest that architecture and surrounding space are meant to be used and enjoyed. Because people can be difficult to draw, however, many designers avoid using them in drawings. The task can be simplified by observation and practice. Trace people from books, magazines, photographs, and slide projections. Compile a tracing file of people with different scale, types of activities, and styles. Then when you need a certain type of figure for a space, you'll have one ready.

People should be matched to the space: children belong in a playground and swimmers around a pool. People also belong in groups or pairs. Several people walking together prevent spottiness and bring realism to the space. Sitting, running, jumping, and bicycling may also be included to generate interest.

Step-by-Step: Figure and Face

1. Draw the eye (horizon) line and assume it is at a five-foot level. Then any object which is drawn from this line down is always five feet tall. For example, the longer light pole in the drawing is actually closer than the shorter one, but they are the same size to the viewer (fig. 6-1). Place each person's eyes on the eye line you have drawn and draw a vertical body line from it. This way people all appear to be on the ground instead of floating or sinking (fig. 6-2). (If the eye line is placed at ten feet or higher, this means that the viewer is elevated and the people will then be positioned so that they are proportionately scaled to five feet tall as in figure 6-3.)

2. To draw a person, project the line slightly above it to allow for the forehead and hair (fig. 6-4). Divide the line in half; the hips are on the halfway point. Divide the distance from the hips to the ground in half. The knees are located at this halfway point. Divide the upper half of the body in half. The shoulders are located at a point slightly more than halfway up the upper half of the body. The elbow and waist are located halfway between the hips and the shoulder.

The chin is established at a point slightly more than halfway down from the distance between the top of the head and the shoulders. The shoulder and the hips are at slight angles, both in opposite directions. The knees and the ankles are parallel to the hips.

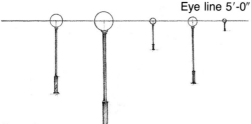

Figure 6-1.

Eye line 5'-0"

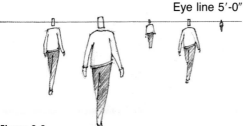

Figure 6-2.

Eye line 5'-0"

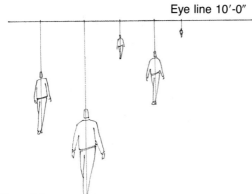

Figure 6-3.

Eye line 10'-0"

Figure 6-4.

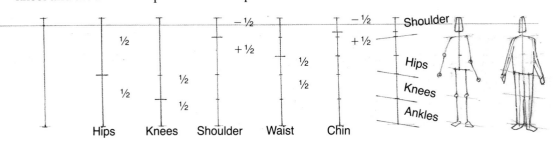

After the elements of the body are located, draw a skeleton figure and build upon it by adding clothes, hair, shoes, etc.

3. Select a figure from your drawing file and position it on the eye line if appropriately sized or use it to copy. Trace or draw the figure in red pencil, then outline in a black felt-tip pen. Remember to be loose in your strokes, and use professional dots and gaps, overlap corners, variable line weight, fuzzy lines, and hit-go-hit lines (figs. 6-5, 6-6).

4. Start coloring in with markers. Use color light and gradual value change, and leave white space. Do not color by numbers but keep the strokes loose and quick. Use color pair and color repeat principles, over-edge, stripes, and dots (fig. 6-7).

5. Add darker values of marker and shade/ shadow. Highlight with colored pencil and a white pen (fig. 6-8).

6. For the face, draw an egg shape, using a continuous, repeat line. Divide it in half to form four quadrants (fig. 6-9). Divide each half of the horizontal line in half again to find the placement of the eyes. Divide each half of the vertical line in half to locate the hairline and position of the nose (fig. 6-10). The ears will fall between the eyes and the nose, and the mouth will fall between the nose and the chin (fig. 6-11).

7. Add further details to the eyes, nose, and mouth, as shown in the example (fig. 6-12). Or omit details and allow a simple T to suggest facial features (6-13).

EXAMPLE: Figures 6-14 to 6-16.

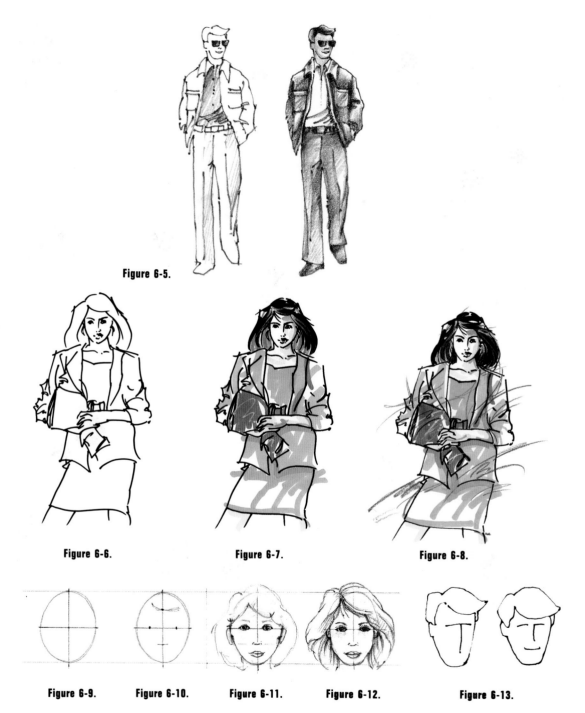

Figure 6-5.

Figure 6-6.   **Figure 6-7.**   **Figure 6-8.**

Figure 6-9.   **Figure 6-10.**   **Figure 6-11.**   **Figure 6-12.**   **Figure 6-13.**

Figure 6-14. Participants, ML Graphic Workshop. Pencil and felt-tip pen on 18" × 24" layout paper. 10 to 30 minutes each.

Figure 6-15. Top Left: Debbie Graviss; top right: Todd Matthews; bottom left: Mansoor Ma, participants, ML Graphic Workshop. Marker, colored pencil, felt-tip pen and pastel on 14″ × 6″ marker paper each. 10 to 40 minutes each. Center, center right, bottom right, participants ML Graphic Workshop. Marker, colored pencil and felt-tip pen on 8″ × 10″ marker paper each. 10 to 30 minutes each.

Figure 6-16. Art Associates, Toledo, OH. Top left: Casein on 5½″ × 7½″ watercolor board. 4 hours. Top center: casein on 2″ × 6″ watercolor board. 1 hour. Right: Gouache on 12″ × 22″ watercolor board. 8 hours. Bottom left: Gouache on 18″ × 18″ water color board. 40 hours.

VEGETATION

Vegetation in plans and elevation drawings gives a sense of scale, is naturalistic, and provides zig-zag and mass/void. It has a variety of forms, shapes, sizes, and colors. Forms can be generally categorized into three basic types: trees, shrubs, and ground covers. Trees and shrubs can be further subdivided into two groups: coniferous (or evergreens) and deciduous.

Technical Tips: Trees in Plan
• Always use a pencil and circle template to rough in trees. Use pens or pencils to outline them later with double circles. This will give the trees a loose, three-dimensional look (fig. 6-17).
• Draw trees approximately ⅔ of their mature size. Avoid making them too large or too small.
• Generally, the smaller the scale of the plan, the more detailed the trees should be. However, this may vary according to the vegetation shown beneath the trees.
• When coloring a tree in plan, use color pair and color next principles and leave some white space (fig. 6-18). When applying color to larger trees that have details underneath, use only light-colored washes.
• When portraying groups of trees in an outline format, use a bold outline around the entire outside perimeter, and a lighter line to define each tree individually (fig. 6-19).
• Always include shadows to differentiate trees from the ground plane and other vegetation. Leave a small white gap between shadow and tree (fig. 6-20). (This can be done with a white colored pencil.)
• When a tree is against a building or over a roof, its shape should always overlap the building.

Figure 6-17.

Figure 6-18.

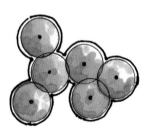

Figure 6-19.

Figure 6-20.

• If hundreds of trees are required, use a stamp that shows a tree. This may be bought from a manufacturer to save time.

Technical Tips: Shrubs and Ground Covers in Plan
• Shrubs should normally be less detailed than trees in plan views. Groups of shrubs are usually represented in a simple outline, with dots for the trunks.
• Deciduous shrubs are usually represented with a smooth outline, evergreens with a jagged edge.
• When rendering, leave some shrubs uncolored or lightly colored to allow for white space.
• Use two line thicknesses when delineating shrubs in outline form, a bold line on the outside and a thinner line on the inside or vice versa.
• It is important to show proper distinction between the grass and ground cover when both are used in the same plan. When applying color or value to ground-cover areas, make sure that it is lighter or darker than both trees and shrubs to allow for differentiation.
• As a rule, ground cover shown directly beneath a tree should be lighter than that in the open.
• Use stripes and dots to create interest in the ground plane.
• When rendering grass on a flat ground plane with marker, use a straightedge to guide the marker.
• Tape two triangles together with a space between them, according to the desired width of the stripe, and use both edges to delineate grass or ground-cover areas (fig. 6-21).

Technical Tips: Trees in Elevation
• Draw trees according to their basic form

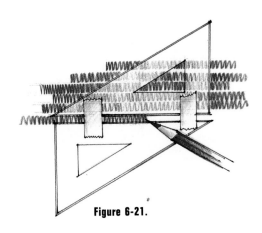

Figure 6-21.

first. These may include round, oval, columnar, irregular, and conical. The outline form alone may be adequate in rough sketches (fig. 6-22).

• Remember to use zig-zag, color pair, and color next principles, and leave some white space. Add dots and finally outline with black.

• Trees behind buildings should be either lighter or darker than the building to create proper contrast.

• Foreground trees should contain the most detail in both the foliage and trunk. Background trees should be shown as simple outlined masses.

• Branching patterns should only be used if elements behind the tree are important to be seen. Trees in full foliage can be used to screen out undesirable views and elements.

• Use concave or convex foliage symbols and letters W or M to show leaf patterns (fig. 6-23).

• Trunks should always be depicted darker directly under the canopy to represent shade and shadow. The overall value of the trunk is highly dependent upon its background. Dark tree trunks should be shown against light backgrounds and vice versa (fig. 6-24).

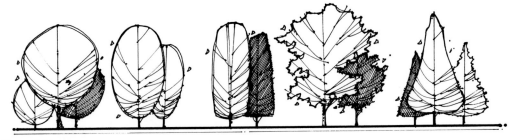

Figure 6-22.

Figure 6-23.

Figure 6-24.

1. Sketch the shape

2. Add light value

3. Add details

Figure 6-25.

Figure 4-33. Eric Hyne, Land Design/Research, Inc., Columbia, MD. Marker, colored pencil, and tempera on 13″ × 20″ blackline diazo print paper (original, pen and ink on vellum). 30 hours.

WATERCOLOR

Watercolor rendering is among the oldest known forms of art and one of the most difficult to master. Watercolor cannot be controlled and corrected the way other media can. However, it is just this uncontrollable spontaneity that makes the medium so exciting. Often, results that look nearly impossible to achieve are no more than accidents that have been accepted and appreciated by the artist.

There are two ways to apply watercolor rendering. One is to use pencil lightly drawn on paper and then render, the other way is to use pen and ink and outline the drawing and then render. The second method is much simpler and gives a rendering a sharp image.

Watercolor rendering skills require practice. Once developed, however, the technique can prove extremely fast, particularly for large wash-type applications such as sky and water. It is also a medium that allows the artist to be relaxed while working.

Materials
Brush no. 3, 8 round, 1-inch flat; frisket material; salt; pocket knife; dish. Winsor & Newton colors: Winsor Blue, Cobalt Blue, Cadmium Red, Cadmium Yellow, Alizarin Crimson, Ivory Black, Burnt Sienna, Raw Sienna, Burnt Umber, Sepia, Thalo Green, Hookers Green (medium).

Step-by-Step
1. Use a pencil and rough in a sketch on tracing paper.
2. Transfer it to an appropriate watercolor paper or board.
3. Use a sharp pencil or pen and ink, if desired, and carefully outline the entire drawing.
4. Start by painting the sky and ground, allowing them to dry totally before any further applications. Build the watercolor slowly, from light to dark.
5. Paint details and entourage.

Technical Tips
- Review and study color principles in chapter 2.
- Proper choice of fine quality paper and brushes is critical. Use brush sizes according to subjects being rendered: large ones for the sky, small ones for details.
- Be prepared for the unpredictable.
- When painting large areas such as the sky and the ground plane, or elements requiring good gradual value change, first apply plain water on the area, wait until the water sheen on paper has vanished, and then immediately apply color. This will prevent undesirable water marks from appearing as you work (fig. 4-34).
- Mix burnt sienna and Hookers green for vegetation, and prussian blue and vermilion for gray tone. Also mix each needed color with burnt umber, gray, or black to achieve color harmony, consistence, and an earthy tone look.
- Use wax pencil, candle wax, or a paper or other frisket to mask off areas and leave appropriate white space.
- Use a sharp tool such as a knife to score the paper and create an interesting texture. To produce a dark texture, score while the paint is wet. For a white highlight, score after paint is dry (fig. 4-35).
- Sprinkle salt on the paper while the surface is still wet to create a special texture as the salt reacts with the water (fig. 4-36).

EXAMPLES: See figures 4-37 to 4-40 for drawings that incorporate the techniques discussed.

Figure 4-34.

Figure 4-35.

Figure 4-36.

1. Rough in a sketch and trace over it in ink.

2. Study value with quick watercolor.

3. Apply with pen and ink.

4. Apply watercolor.

Figure 4-37.

Figure 4-38. Robert Hanna, Lincoln, NE. Pen and ink and watercolor on 10″ × 12″ watercolor paper each. 1 hour each.

Figure 4-39. Top: Jay Kabriel, Annapolis, MD. Watercolor on 18″ × 24″ watercolor paper each. 6 hours each. Bottom left: Gary Mellenbruch, Kansas City, MO. Watercolor on 22″ × 30″ watercolor board. 14 hours. Bottom right: Dick Sneary, Kansas City, MO. Watercolor on 16″ × 20″ watercolor paper (original pen and ink on vellum). 13 to 15 hours.

Figure 4-40. Top left, bottom left: Dick Sneary, Susan Lynn, Kansas City, MO. Watercolor on 7″ × 9″ watercolor paper (original, pen and ink on vellum). 15 to 20 hours. Top right: Dick Sneary, Vern Christiansen, Kansas City, MO. Watercolor on 12″ × 16″ photomural paper (original, pen and ink on vellum). 20 hours. Bottom right: Dick Sneary, Vern Christiansen, Kansas City, MO. Watercolor on 7″ × 9″ watercolor paper (original, pen and ink on vellum). 20 hours.

TEMPERA

Tempera, unlike watercolor, is an opaque water-based medium. Its opaque characteristic makes it much easier to control than watercolor, as it allows the artist to make corrections. It can also be used as a supplementary medium to any of the other colored media, particularly marker. It is excellent for adding details and entourage such as figures, cars, and vegetation. And it may be applied to a variety of surfaces including boards and specific papers.

When using tempera, always attempt to move from the background to the foreground to avoid masking areas off. When doing detail areas, however, masking may be necessary to prevent the surrounding area from being painted. This requires a lot of time and also demands much practice as a beginner.

Materials
Brush no. 3, 8 round; ¼″, ⅜″, 1″, and 2″ flat; tape; Pelican graphic white; Winsor & Newton Watercolor Blue; Designers Gouache: Burnt Sienna, Burnt Umber, Jet Black, Grenadine, Permanent Green Deep, Golden Yellow, Lemon Yellow.

Step-by-Step
1. Use a pencil and rough in a sketch on paper. Transfer the sketch with carbon paper to an illustration board. Use frisket materials to mask off buildings, roads, parking areas, and so on. Use an acrylic medium to paint the sky and ground planes. Acrylics are tough and cannot be easily damaged (fig. 4-41).
2. Peel the entire frisket off, place a new frisket over the drawing, lifting off areas that now need to be painted, such as building, windows, a roof top, and so on.

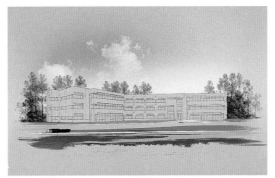
1. Transfer sketch onto illustration board and render sky, background, and foreground.

2. Render the building.

3. Add middleground tree and foreground detail.

4. Add entourage.
Figure 4-41.

3. Repeat the above step to render a parking lot and other areas, such as middleground and foreground detail.
4. Finally, add the necessary entourage including people, vegetation, cars, a fountain, and so on.

Technical Tips:
• Use a vignette approach on colored board. For example, if you are painting a beige building choose a beige-colored board, so that a portion of the building need not be painted.
• Start painting from the background to the foreground. Apply darker values toward foreground.
• Use acrylic as a medium to paint large

areas such as grass foreground. This will allow for wear during the painting process and prevent water marks should water drip on the drawing.
• Use the combination of airbrush and pastel for the sky to achieve a more realistic look.
• Apply thin rubber cement with a wide brush to very thin frosted acetate paper to produce the frisket paper.
• Make a T-bar bridge to draw straight lines with a brush. An architect's scale may be used.

EXAMPLES: See figures 4-42 to 4-44 for drawings that incorporate the techniques discussed.

Figure 4-42. Art Associates, Toledo, OH. Casein on 12" × 20" watercolor board. 30 hours.

Figure 4-43. Left: Art Associates, Toledo, OH. Casein on 16″ × 22″ watercolor board. 50 hours. Right: Gary Mellenbruch, Kansas City, MO. Tempera on 28″ × 36″ illustration board. 30 hours.

Figure 4-44. Prelim & Associates, Dallas, TX. Gouache on 18″ × 24″ illustration board. 48 hours.

Airbrush

Airbrush techniques represent perhaps the most sophisticated form of tone or color application. The airbrush mixes pigment and water with air to produce a fine mist or spray. Value change here is controlled by air and pigment dispersion, allowing for very consistent value changes.

Airbrush rendering requires both time and patience. Areas must be carefully masked before and during application. If the airbrush is used properly, however, this technique produces very realistic drawings.

Regular airbrush techniques produce tone values without an outline, but airbrushing outlined drawings is much easier to learn. The quick drying characteristics, combined with its realistic look, make the airbrush very suitable for architectural rendering.

In general, there are two types of airbrushes available: single action and double action. A single-action airbrush is one with a single trigger which is pressed down to emit both pigment and air. The farther down the trigger is depressed, the more air and pigment are released, thus the darker the value produced. A double-action airbrush has a trigger which when depressed emits air only. With the double-action air brush, pigment is added by pulling back on the trigger. The double-action air brush is of a much

higher quality and is recommended for the optimum results.

Air sources may be obtained either in bottled or canned compressed air, or an actual compressor.

Materials

Airbrush set by Bager #100, Passche VL, or Thayer Chandler Model A; air brush ink, watercolor, or Designers Gouache; air compressor, propellant, or spray kit by Eberhard Faber; frisket materials; x-acto knife; tape.

Step-by-Step: Rendering a Cube

1. Use pencil to sketch a cube. If paper is being used, it should be mounted on a foam-core board to avoid warping.
2. Lay a big frisket over the entire cube and with an x-acto knife, cut lightly along the lines of the cube. Some sketches can be drawn directly on the frisket paper, so that no line will show on the finished drawing.
3. Start by lifting frisket paper from the darkest area needed and airbrush lightly (fig. 4-45).
4. Lift the frisket paper from next lighter area, and spray it and the first area together. The darkest area has now received two coats (fig. 4-46).
5. Repeat this process (fig. 4-47) until the lightest area is sprayed (fig. 4-48). If there are four different valued areas, the lightest

area will receive one coat where the darkest area will receive four coats. This procedure will not only use one sheet of frisket paper, but prevent undesirable white lines caused by cutting different frisket paper.

Technical Tips

• Apply values evenly and slowly. For any given air pressure, the closer to the surface of the drawing, the darker the values will be. It is always recommended to start farther away from the drawing, working toward it, unless details are required.
• Apply the spray 3 to 5 inches beyond the left and right of an object to obtain an even value.
• Use low tack, or frisket which is easily cut, applied, and removed. Also nonopaque frisket allows you to see the original surface.
• When masking, always be sure to cover a sufficient area. The fine mist emitted from the airbrush may spray beyond the frisket into undesired areas. Tempera and gouache are recommended for beginners.
• The airbrush should be cleaned after each use. This will prolong its life.

EXAMPLES: See figures 4-49 and 4-50 for drawings that incorporate the techniques discussed.

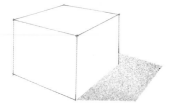

Figure 4-45.

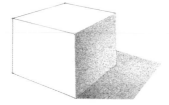

Figure 4-46.

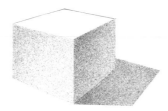

Figure 4-47.

Figure 4-48.

Figure 4-49. Dick Sneary, Kansas City, MO. Airbrush on 20″ × 30″ brown sepia print (original, pen and ink on vellum). 85 hours.

Figure 4-50. Dick Sneary, Kansas City, MO. Airbrush on 24′′′′ × 36′′ photomural paper (original, pen and ink on vellum). 175 hours.

MEDIA COMPARISON

In each of the examples (figs. 4-51 to 4-53) the same subject is rendered in different media. Studying the quality of this work will help you to select the medium appropriate to whatever subject you have. The building study (fig. 4-54) is rendered in all twenty rendering techniques and twenty-seven rendering types. This overview widens the selection appropriate to your presentation.

MATRIX CHART

The matrix (fig. 4-55) provides a simple way to evaluate rendering techniques and types. Located on different sides of the matrix, each has been subdivided: rendering techniques into "how to see," "how to draw," and "how to apply," while media types are categorized according dry, semiwet, and wet. Each rendering technique and media type has been cross-referenced to the others. Techniques and media types are individually examined. A red dot identifies the best technique for any media types. Areas within the matrix left blank are either marginal or not applicable.

Time requirements, client satisfaction, skill level, and the value of the illustration are identified for each respective technique and media type. For example, to evaluate a continuous-line technique, the most suitable rendering types are pencil, pastel, ink, and marker. Then study time involved, client's satisfaction, skill level required, and value of rendering, listed in the same column.

This matrix chart is a guide, not a hard-and-fast rule. Do not let it stop you from experimenting on your own.

Figure 4-51. Dick Sneary, Kansas City, MO. Felt-tip pen, pastel, colored pencil, and watercolor on 8″ × 10″ marker paper, and watercolor paper respectively. 1 hour each.

Figure 4-53. Top: Chad Moor, participant, ML Graphic Workshop. Pencil and felt-tip pen on 11″×15″ bond paper each. 30 minutes each. Bottom left: Dick Sneary, Kansas City, MO. Colored pencil on 11″×15″ marker paper. 1 hour. Bottom right: Patricia Marovich, participant, ML Graphic Workshop. Pastel on 11″×15″ marker paper. 1 hour.

Follow these three steps in rendering trees: (1) sketch the outline, (2) add light color and outline with black, (3) add darker and more colors with details (fig. 6-25).

Technical Tips: Shrubs and Ground Covers in Elevation

• Both deciduous and evergreen shrubs may be classified into round, creeping, outlined, branched, and branched with outline (fig. 6-26).

• Follow the principles outlined for drawing trees in elevation.

• In a marker rendering, use opaque tempera and paint over the marker to add shrubs.

• Usually foreground grass should be darker than background unless a focal point is needed in the center.

• Add stripes and black or white dots to create interest and add texture to the grass.

• When rendering the grass in color, include color pair and color next principles to create interest and a realistic appearance.

• When using short strokes to show grass in perspective, the distance between strokes should gradually widen toward the foreground. Their angle determines the flat or rolling nature of the ground plane (fig. 6-27).

EXAMPLES: Figures 6-28 to 6-30.

Figure 6-26.

Figure 6-27

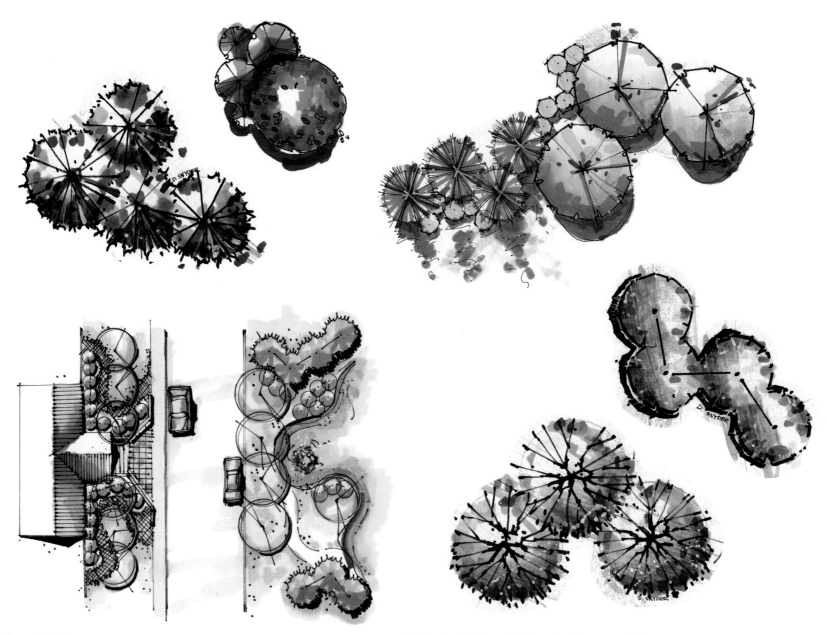

Figure 6-28. Top, bottom right: Deanna Snyder; bottom left: Thaddeus Yonke, participants, ML Graphic Workshop. Marker, colored pencil, and felt-tip pen on 8″ × 10″ marker paper each. 20 minutes to 1 hour each.

Figure 6-29. Center left: Larry Wegkamp; center: Thomas White; bottom left: Tai Kim-Eng; bottom center, bottom right: Shelly Stephenson; top left, top right, participants, ML Graphic Workshop. Marker, colored pencil, and felt-tip pen on 6″ × 10″ marker paper each. 10 to 25 minutes each.

Figure 6-30. Top left, bottom left: Nancy Ewalt; bottom right: Marie-Claued Seguin; top right, top center, participants, ML Graphic Workshop. Marker, colored pencil, and felt-tip pen on 10″ × 12″ marker paper each. 10 to 20 minutes each.

CARS

The inclusion of cars in a drawing adds scale, activity, and realism. Cars also help to create a good composition, hide undesirable elements, complement the space, and add prestige.

Although it is a good idea to collect pictures of cars from magazines, books, and dealership brochures for detail reference, cars must never be traced in a drawing. It is too time consuming to find just the right car for the scale of the drawing, at just the right angle. Most traced cars appear to be tilted, digging into or taking off from streets.

Choose cars appropriate to the nature of the project. Expensive cars will add to the prestige of a rendering. Draw cars traveling in both directions as well as turning, if possible. Remember to include people driving the cars.

Always add shadows of cars on the street. The detail level of the car should be comparable to the complexity of the drawing. The color used on the car can be a color that complements the rest of the drawing, such as a red car against green scenery or an orange car against blue sky.

Step-by-Step

1. *Draw and trisect a cube.* According to the lines of the perspective, draw a cube approximately sixteen feet long, six feet wide, and four and a half feet high. Trisect the cube into three horizontal portions, with line A being the top of the hood and trunk, and line B showing the approximate location of bumpers (fig. 6-31).

2. *Draw the cab.* On line A, locate point a and b as the length of cab (normally slightly longer than ⅓ of line A). Construct a three dimensional cab by projecting lines from points a and b to obtain points c, d, e, f, g, h.

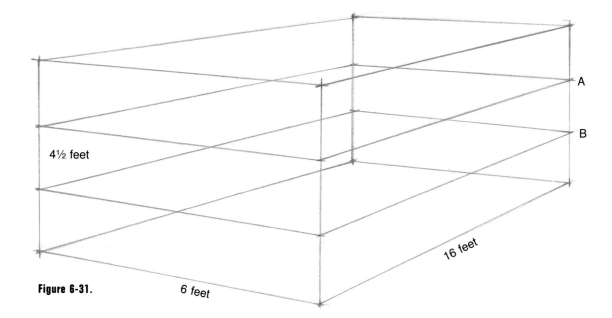

Figure 6-31.

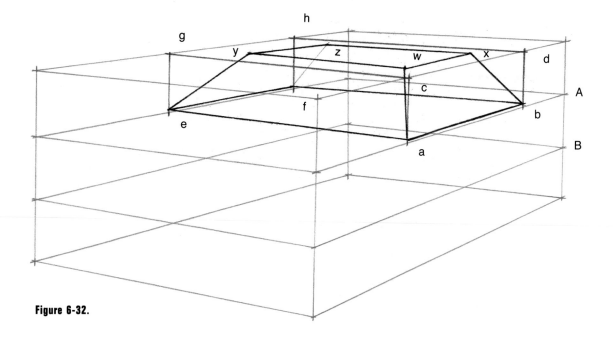

Figure 6-32.

Recess slightly from points c, d, g, h to get points w, x, y, and z, to form the top of the cab. Then connect points w to a, x to b, y to e, and z to f. This completes the cab of the car (fig. 6-32).

3. *Draw the car.* From the base of the windshields points a, e, and b, f, gently angle downward toward the front and the back to create the hood and trunk. Draw front and rear bumpers accordingly. Note that the base of the car (line C) should be lower than line B (fig. 6-33).

4. *Draw the wheels.* Locate the front wheel well next to the front bumper and position a vertical and horizontal axis in 90 degrees. Locate four points of a wheel shape and draw the wheel with repeat and continuous line, or an elliptical template. Draw the rear wheel using the same method. Remember to include the width of the wheel (fig. 6-34).

5. *Add the details.* Details of the car may now be added. These can include doors, lights, molding, the grill, and other desired features. Use a car brochure if needed (fig. 6-35).

EXAMPLES: Figures 6-36 and 6-37.

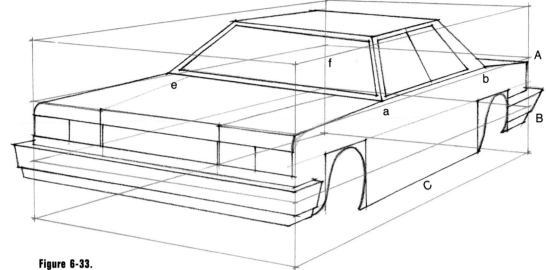

Figure 6-33.

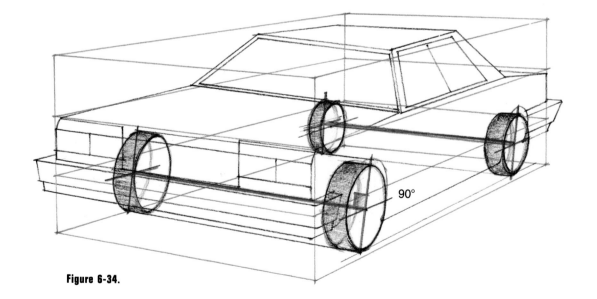

Figure 6-34.

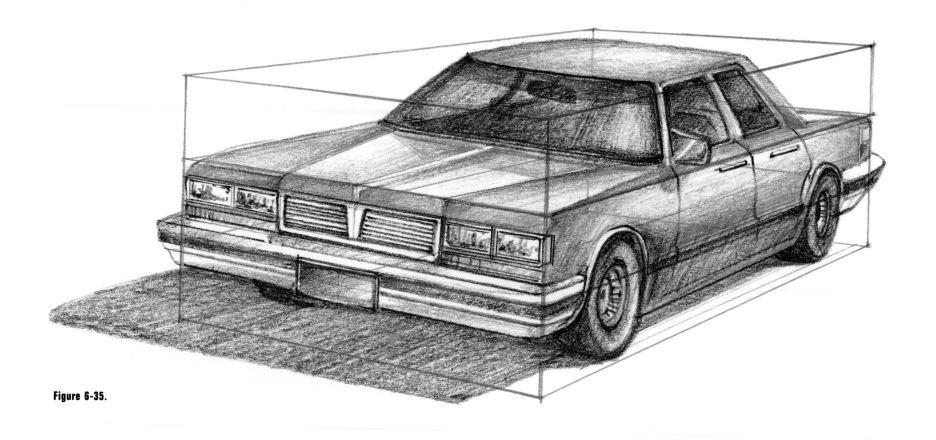

Figure 6-35.

Figure 6-36. Top left: Marie-Claued Seguin; top right, center: Debbie Graviss; bottom left: Richard Berry; bottom right: Alan Kato, participants, ML Graphic Workshop. Marker, color pencil, and felt-tip pen on 4″ × 8″ to 7″ × 14″ marker paper. 20 to 50 minutes each.

Figure 6-37. Top left: participant, ML Graphic Workshop; bottom right: Kathy Heimerman, participant, ML Graphic Workshop. Marker, colored pencil, and tempera on trimmed 7″ × 14″ marker paper each, pasted over black construction paper. 6 hours each. Top right, bottom left: Art Associates, Toledo, OH. Casein on 2½″ × 5″ watercolor board. 3 hours each.

FURNITURE

Furniture creates a zig-zag composition and mass/void, and sets the mood of the interior. Prestigious furniture adds status to the drawing; in awkward, ugly spaces, problems can be camouflaged by strategic placement of furniture.

Technical Tips
• Never trace furniture in a rendering. Assume the form of the furniture is within the cube or box shape and place it in the perspective. Then draw the furniture in the cube and add the necessary details (fig. 6-38).
• Use a red pencil to rough it out first and then outline it with a black felt-tip pen (fig. 6-39). Use light tones for the fabric and color quickly, leaving white space and using color pair. Immediately add darker values to achieve gradual value change. Add shade/shadow, and highlight with colored pencil and marker stripes. Compile a furniture file of photographs cut from magazines and furniture catalogs. It is helpful to have a file on name-brand furniture for your reference. From it you can choose furniture appropriate to the decor and style of the space. It should fit the image you are trying to convey. Place furniture in groups. Random spacing may cause spottiness in the overall composition. When rendering, remember to use color pair, gradual value change, shade/shadow, dots, and stripes. Because of the complexity of upholstery textures and colors, many people "color by numbers" when rendering furniture. This can produce a spotty effect. There are actually many colors and patterns that, when combined, create a very pleasing piece.

EXAMPLES: Figures 6-40 and 6-41.

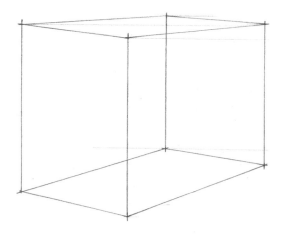

Figure 6-38.

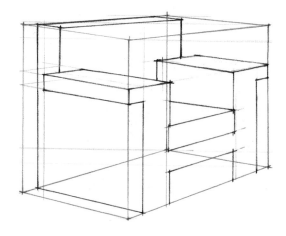

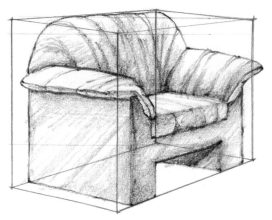

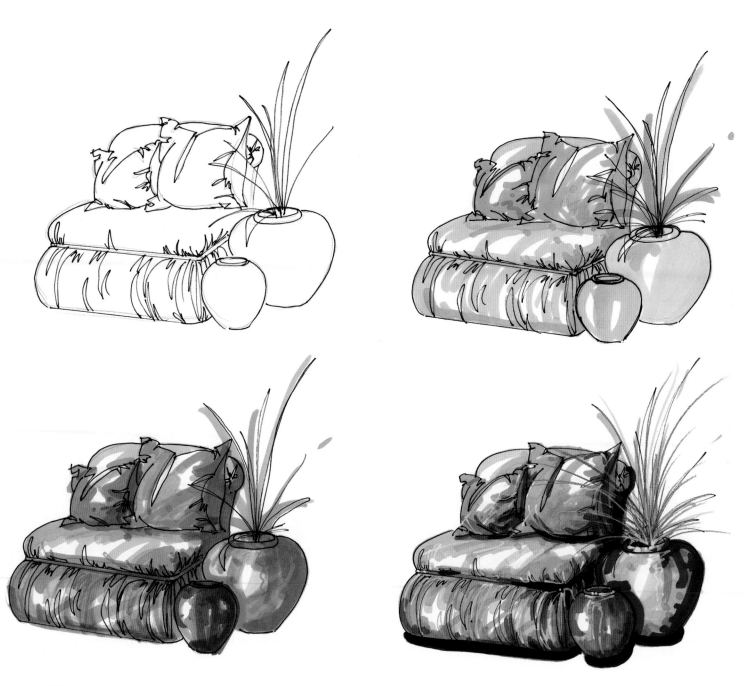

Figure 6-39. Step-by-step of how to color a chair.

Figure 6-40. Top: participants, ML Graphic Workshop. Marker and felt-tip pen on 8″ × 20″ marker paper. 30 minutes. Bottom: Debbie Graviss, participant, ML Graphic Workshop. Marker, colored pencil, and felt-tip pen on 10″ × 20″ marker paper. 40 minutes.

Figure 6-41. Debbie Graviss, illustrator, Lexington, KY. Marker, colored pencil, and felt-tip pen on 19″×24″ marker paper. 30 minutes to 1 hour each.

SKIES

The sky comprises a large part of a drawing and can set the overall mood of the space, from sunny to stormy, sunset to midnight. It can help to balance the drawing and focus attention on your subject.

The shapes of clouds are often used to obtain a good zig-zag composition. Generally, light colors will soften the drawing and not draw attention away from the focal point. Use of the color pair helps to excite and enhance the overall color scheme. Too much color, however, will make the sky look muddy and unreal.

Technical Tips
• Always work on the sky first when rendering in ink, watercolor, or tempera, and last when rendering in pencil, pastel, and marker.
• Sky treatment should not overpower the rest of the drawing, but should reinforce the composition. A drawing may be ruined by overworking the sky. Keep it simple, remembering the principle of "less is more."
• When laying out the shape of a sky, keep it in a zig-zag formation and do not follow the outer edge of buildings. After all, the sky is always behind the building, not on top of it (fig. 6-42).
• The color of the sky should meet the horizon line and/or the buildings, so the elements on the ground will not appear to be floating. As a rule, the sky should always get lighter as it reaches the horizon line. However, in quick sketches, the sky may need to be darker toward the center of a drawing and lighter as it proceeds outward to create focal point and achieve mass/void against a light-colored building. Using orange color near the horizon will add excitement by color pairing.

• When coloring a sky, use the same medium as in the rest of the drawing to help maintain consistency. Certain media such as markers may have limitations for large areas because of its stroke appearance. In that case, use pastel, for example, for the sky.
• Use a knife and scrape a blue pastel stick to create powder and deposit it on desired areas. With your finger tip, push upward and away from a building to create the appearance of sky. Add white pastel over the blue to create clouds (fig. 6-43).

EXAMPLES: Figures 6-44 and 6-45.

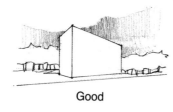

Good   Bad

Figure 6-42.

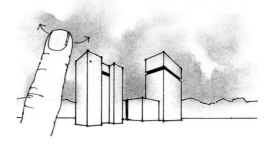

Figure 6-43.

Figure 6-44. Participants, ML Graphic Workshop. Pencil, colored pencil, ink, pastel, marker, and airbrush on 4″×6″ copy paper each. 5 to 15 minutes each.

Figure 6-45. Top: participants, ML Graphic Workshop. Pastel and tempera on 11″ × 18″ mat board each. 30 minutes each. Bottom: Art Associates, Toledo OH. Casein on 8″ × 10″ watercolor board each. 3 to 10 hours each.

WATER

Water is usually included in a design as an enticing amenity. A placid lake conveys a sense of tranquility, while an enormous fountain suggests excitement. Many successful projects have included water features for such reasons.

Water elements range from reflecting pools, swimming pools and lakes, to fountains, waterfalls, and rivers. Here we will explore standing and moving water in both plans and sketches.

Technical Tips: Standing Water
• Use vertical strokes to represent reflected surfaces and horizontal strokes to show smooth, mirrored surfaces.
• After applying appropriate vertical or horizontal strokes to the water surfaces, use a white pastel or a white colored pencil over the previous strokes in the opposite direction to render reflection.
• In a plan view of a pool rendered in pastel, use a kneaded eraser at a 45-degree angle to break up the surface and create reflections. If the pool is rendered in marker, a white pastel should be used.
• Use pastel or airbrush to cover large areas such as lakes. Add shadows to convey a sense of depth.
• Blend to make a gradual value change in the water surface. In sketches, always apply darker value toward the background.
• Include other types of entourage with the water to give it a lifelike appearance: people swimming in the water, or boats sailing on the lake. Use color pair principles such as people wearing orange or red bathing suits against blue water.

Technical Tips: Moving Water
• Apply similar key techniques described in standing water.
• Use different sizes of bubbles, black and white dots, and curved lines to suggest waves and ripples as well as add interest and movement to the water.
• Keep fountains or waterfalls in white or lighter color against darker background and vice versa. This will give the drawing a good mass/void.

• The vertical surface of a fountain or waterfall should be a lighter value and the horizontal plane should be darker in order to achieve depth and dark/light effect.
• Maintain a thin white space along the shore line to separate the water from the ground, either by leaving white space or using a white colored pencil.

EXAMPLES: Figures 6-46 and 6-47.

Figure 6-46. Top left: Scott Arbogast; top right: Steve Wikner; bottom right: Chad Moor; bottom left, participants, ML Graphic Workshop. Marker and colored pencil on 8″ × 12″ marker paper each. 10 to 30 minutes each.

Figure 6-47. Top left, bottom: Art Associates, Toledo, OH. Casein on 2″ × 5″ to 3″ × 5″ watercolor board each. 4 hours each. Top right: Dick Sneary, Kansas City, MO. Watercolor on 10″ × 10″ watercolor paper (original, pen and ink on vellum). 3 hours.

GLASS

Most buildings include glass in one form or another. Glass itself comes in a multitude of types: transparent or colored, smoked or mirrored. One of the best ways to learn to render glass is to study professional illustrations.

Step-by-Step

1. To draw a mullioned-glass window, first render the glass as a single sheet, with gradual value change (fig. 6-48).
2. Apply shadow of the mullion on glass.
3. Use an appropriate opaque color to draw the mullion over its shadow area. This will save time because you will not need to add shadow to each mullion. Also study the glass renderings in figure 6-49.

Technical Tips

• If at all possible, create gradual value change when depicting windows to create interest.
• When drawing transparent or semi-transparent glass, try to show objects inside the window to create realism. These may include ceiling or indoor lights, curtains, people, and plants.
• When drawing reflective glass, include elements from the neighboring environment such as sky, vegetation, and people.
• Windows on the sunny side of the building should be darker than those on the shaded side. This creates contrast and mass/void.
• When using watercolor to render glass, wet the entire window area before applying color.

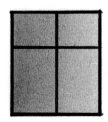
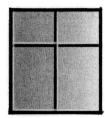

Figure 6-48.

Figure 6-49. Gary Mellenbruch, Kansas City, MO. Tempera on 28″ × 36″ illustration board each. 14 hours each.

BUILDING MATERIALS

An understanding of man-made materials and how to render them is essential to architectural drawing. Materials include wood, brick, tile, stone, concrete, rock, metal, and glass. The success of a rendering can rest on the quality of its details. Careful observation and as much practice as you can allow will help you to develop your skills.

Technical Tips
• When rendering materials, always include gradual value change and color pair, and leave some white space.
• Add stripes, dots, shade and shadow to the appropriate surfaces to create interest.
• After the basic color of the object is completed, add details and highlights with colored pencils.

EXAMPLES: Figures 6-50 to 6-53.

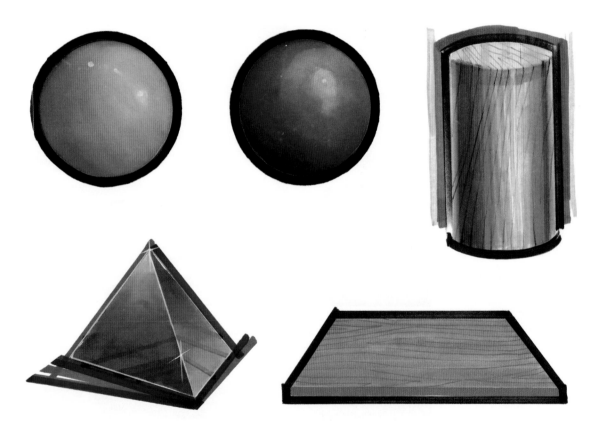

Figure 6-50. Top left, center, bottom left: Brian Fisher; top right, bottom right: Steve Roark, participants, ML Graphic Workshop. Marker and colored pencil on 19″ × 24″ marker paper. 10 to 25 minutes each.

Figure 6-51. Top left, bottom right: Ronald Kemnitzer, Kansas City, MO. Marker and colored pencil on 9″ × 14″ marker paper each. 35 minutes each. Top center, top right: participant, ML Graphic Workshop. Marker on 3″ × 5″ bond paper each, bottom left. Bottom center, participants, ML Graphic Workshop. Marker and colored pencil on 8″ × 12″ marker paper each. 10 to 30 minutes each.

Figure 6-52. Shannon Gordon, participant, ML Graphic Workshop. Marker and felt-tip pen on 8″ × 12″ marker paper each. 20 minutes each.

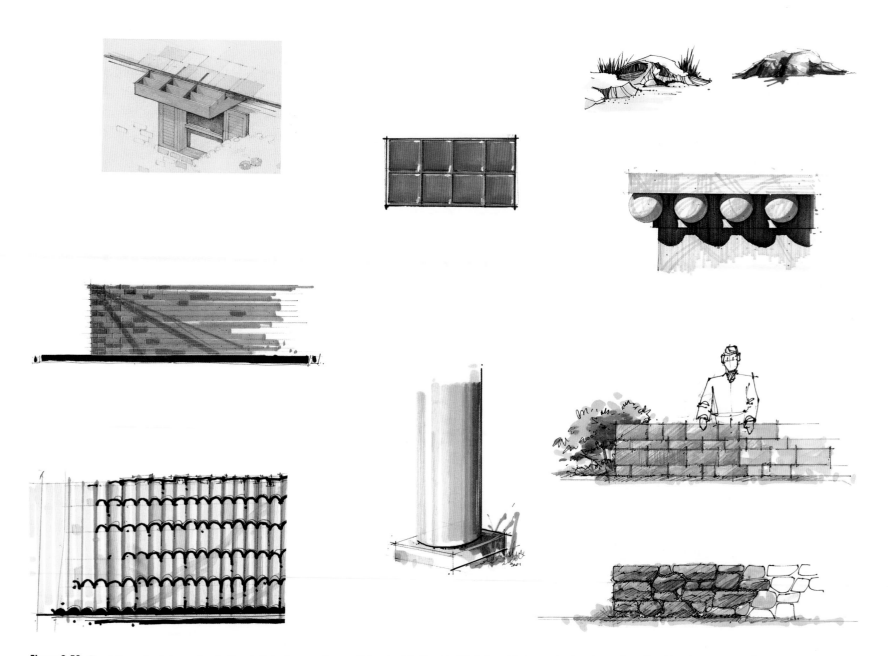

Figure 6-53. Top left, center left, center, bottom left, bottom center: participants, ML Graphic Workshop. Marker and colored pencil on 5″ × 8″ marker paper each. 20 minutes each. Top center, top right: Jean Kavanagh, participant, ML Graphic Workshop. Marker and felt-tip pen on 5″ × 10″ marker paper each. 10 minutes each. Bottom right: Scott Collard, participant, ML Graphic Workshop. Marker, colored pencil and felt-tip pen on 8″ × 10″ marker paper. 30 minutes.

7. 永 PERSPECTIVE DRAWING

A perspective drawing is a three-dimensional view translated in two dimensions. It is an excellent way to evaluate a design concept. The proposed architecture for a space may be seen in context and possible design problems may be dealt with early in the process. The realism and lifelike imagery of perspectives allow the client to understand the finished product better and may help to sell the design.

In the study of perspective, there are several terms, or concepts, that are fundamental (fig. 7-1).

horizon line, or **"eye line":** The line where the viewer's eye is located. It is also the distance from the viewer's eyes to the ground line.

picture plane: A theoretical, transparent plane upon which the image of the object is projected and a perspective is drawn.

ground line: The meeting place of picture plane and ground.

vanishing point: The point on the horizon line at which parallel lines converge. Parallel lines, such as the edges of a road, as they recede in the distance appear to meet, a phenomenon with which we are all familiar.

station point: The point from which the observer views the object.

cone of vision: An imaginary circle that represents the view of the object or space that your eye may see in an undistorted manner.

There are three types of perspectives: one-point, two-point, and three-point perspective (fig. 7-2). In **one-point perspective**

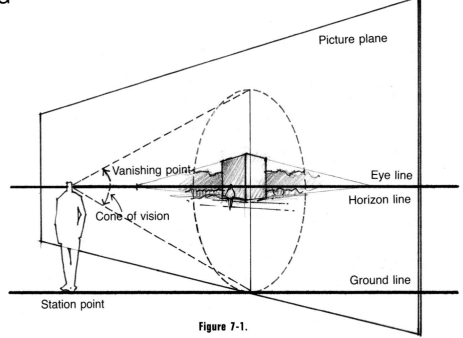

Figure 7-1.

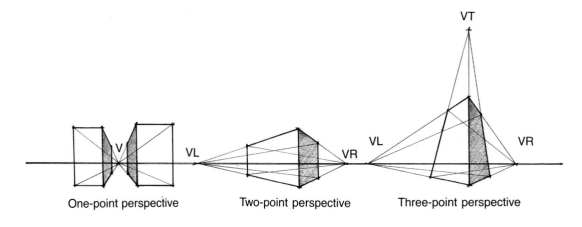

One-point perspective   Two-point perspective   Three-point perspective

Figure 7-2.

the viewer is parallel to the space in front of him, and there is one vanishing point from which all lines in the drawing originate. In **two-point perspective** the viewer is at an angle to the building or space in front of him. There are two vanishing points for all lines of a building—a right and a left one. **Three-point perspective** is seldom used because in nature it is rarely seen. It is similar to two-point perspective, but the viewer's head is tilted back, as though looking up at a skyscraper.

The height from which the viewer looks at a building or object will determine the type of view (fig. 7-3). A worm's-eye view is from the ground level or below it. It is not a very common perspective. The view at eye level is a typical and realistic perspective, because it is the way we generally view our surroundings. Finally, the view from above an object is called a bird's-eye view. This is a good way to show an entire project.

Before you can draw a perspective, you must be able to plot height, width, and depth. Using the following methods, a designer can draw a perspective quickly and therefore design three-dimensional spaces more effectively.

HEIGHT IN PERSPECTIVE
STACKING METHOD

The fundamental principle of this method is that lines drawn down from the eye line in any length will be read as equal in height. For example, in figure 7-4 the people standing in a field are all 5 feet tall. Every person's eyes are on the same line, the eye line. The larger people are closer to the viewer. Once this principle is understood and the height of the eye line is determined, the stacking method can be used to measure the height of an object.

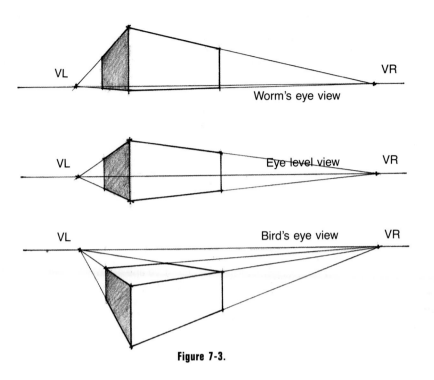

Worm's eye view

Eye level view

Bird's eye view

Figure 7-3.

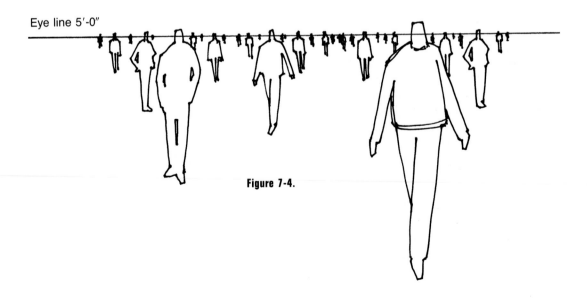

Eye line 5'-0"

Figure 7-4.

Step-by-Step

1. Draw an eye line and assume it is at a 5-foot level (fig. 7-5).

2. Draw a person down from the eye line at any spot. Now you can double the person's length to achieve a 10-foot height, or triple the length to reach 15 feet (fig. 7-6). You must add on above the eyeline.

3. If the eye line is at a 10-foot level, (which means the viewer is standing on a 5-foot object) any line drawn down from the eye line is 10 feet tall. Therefore stack two people to reach the 10-foot eye line, stack four for a 20-foot tall tree, or stack six to get a 30-foot tall building (fig. 7-7).

4. Using the same principle, if the eye line is at a 40-foot level, any spot on the ground to the eye line will be 40 feet tall, or double it to achieve an 80-foot tall height (fig. 7-8).

INCREMENT METHOD

This method is used to find the height of an object in perspective. In the example (fig. 7-9), we will locate an 8-foot flagpole and a 3½-foot post.

Step-by-Step

1. Draw an eye line at a 5-foot level.

2. Pick a point A, where the flagpole is to be located, and draw a vertical line upward.

3. Select one edge of an engineer's scale and place its 0 on point A. Position the scale so the numeral 5 on the same scale can reach the eye line. (The angle of the scale has no bearing, and if the eye line is 6 feet, place the numeral 6 on it.)

4. Draw a horizontal line (line 1) from the numeral 8 to intersect at point B with the vertical line previously drawn to establish the height of the 8-foot flagpole.

5. Pick a point X, where the 3½-foot post is to be located, and draw a vertical line up-

Eye line 5'-0"

Figure 7-5.

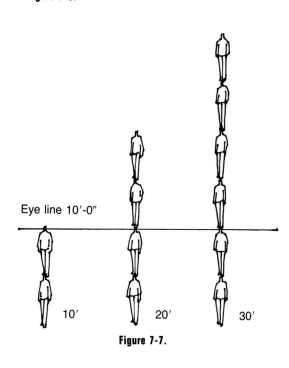

Eye line 10'-0"

10'   20'   30'

Figure 7-7.

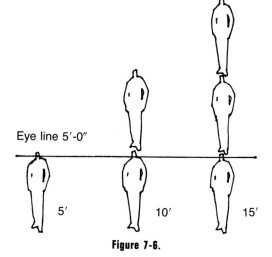

Eye line 5'-0"

5'   10'   15'

Figure 7-6.

Eye line 40'-0"

40'   80'

Figure 7-8.

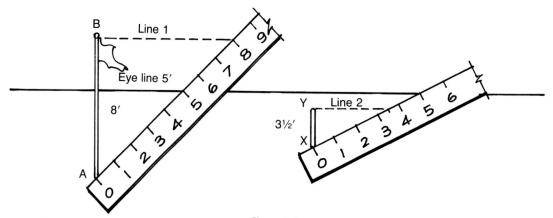

B   Line 1

Eye line 5'

8'

A

Y   Line 2

3½'

X

Figure 7-9.

ward. Select another edge of the scale and place its 0 on point X and 5 on the eye line. From point 3.5 on the scale, draw a line (line 2) parallel to the eye line, and intersect with the vertical line at Y to find a 3½-foot post.

PROJECTION METHOD

Projection is used to find the specific height of an object from another object with a known height. Here, a flagpole with a given height of 8 feet is used to find another flagpole of the same height in a different location (fig. 7-10).

Step-by-Step

1. Draw an eye line at a 5-foot level, and an 8-foot flagpole, AB. Locate point C at an appropriate spot as the base of another flagpole.
2. Draw a vertical line up from point C.
3. Connect C to A, and extend it to E on the eye line.
4. Connect E through B, and intersect with the vertical line previously drawn from point C, thus creating point D.
5. CD is therefore another flagpole 8 feet tall.
6. The same method can be used to find the height of any 8-foot flagpole located anywhere on the ground (fig. 7-11).
7. If the two flagpoles are located almost the same distance from the viewer, this method will not be appropriate. Other methods may be used more effectively.

RUBBER BAND METHOD

This method is not as accurate as the others but is an easy way to obtain the approximate height of an object.

Step-by-Step

1. Stretch a wide rubber band and draw 10 or more small, evenly spaced horizontal

marks with a very thin felt-tip pen.
2. Stretch the marked rubber band and place it vertically so that its first mark is located at point A, and fifth mark is on the eye line (fig. 7-12).
3. The eighth mark will be the height of the flagpole, and the mark at 3½ will be the height of the post.

WIDTH IN PERSPECTIVE

In the following examples, it is assumed that the eye line is at a 5-foot level.

To find a 5-foot wide line within a space (fig. 7-13):

Step-by-Step

1. Draw an eye line at a 5-foot level.
2. At any spot, draw a 5-foot height line, AB, down vertically from the eye line.
3. From point B, draw a line BC parallel to the eye line. Then from point A, draw a 45-degree line to intersect at C. Line BC is 5 feet wide.

To find a 20-foot wide space (fig. 7-14):

Step-by-Step

1. Draw an eye line at a 5-foot level.
2. Draw a person 5 feet tall on the left side of the drawing. Locate the person's eyes on the eye line, and the feet close to the bottom edge of the paper.
3. Draw a ground line toward the right side of the paper, starting from the person's feet.
4. Use the height of the person for 5-foot horizontal increments along the ground line to achieve a 20-foot width of the space.

It is advisable to draw the ground line first, and decide the total length of the line to fit the width of the drawing. Then find a 5-foot length of that ground line to establish

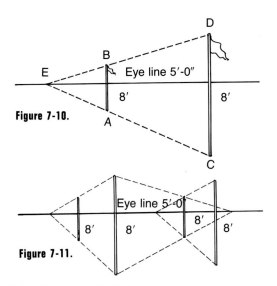

Figure 7-10.

Figure 7-11.

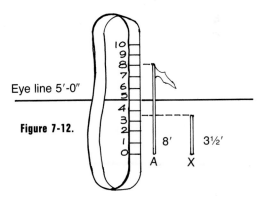

Figure 7-12.

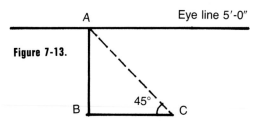

Figure 7-13.

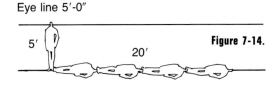

Figure 7-14.

the person's height and transfer this dimension vertically to find the eye line. This will help you to control the size of the drawing from the beginning (explained in more detail in the one-point perspective quick method).

DEPTH IN PERSPECTIVE

The person drawing the perspective is the viewer and can stand any distance away from an imaginary glass plane called the picture plane and draw on the glass what is seen through it. This is a perspective drawing.

Let us assume that the viewer is standing 20 feet from the picture plane (fig. 7-15) and will draw an object located 20 feet behind the glass. This object will appear in the middle of the eye and ground lines in the perspective drawing. In other words, the distance from the halfway point, the point between the eye and ground lines, to the ground line can be any depth as long as it is equal to the distance from the ground line to the viewer (fig. 7-16).

For example, in figure 7-17, the viewer stands in front of a floor-length mirror and places a strip of masking tape horizontally on the bottom of the mirror to represent the ground line. Another strip of tape 5 feet above the floor is the eye line (assume the viewer is 5 feet tall), and a third strip of tape 2½ feet above the floor is the halfway point between the ground and eye lines. The viewer will soon notice that regardless of how far or close he is standing from the mirror, his shoes in the mirror will always appear at the halfway point.

There are several ways to find depth in a one-point perspective drawing. (In these examples, it is assumed that a 5-foot person is standing 20 feet away from the ground

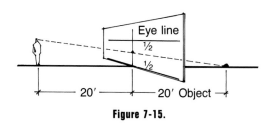

Figure 7-15.

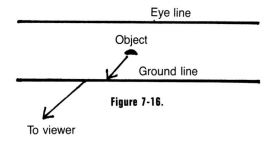

Figure 7-16.

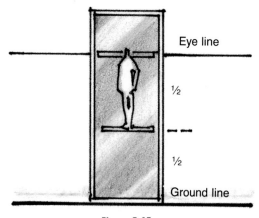

Figure 7-17.

line/picture plane.) Use one method to cross-check another method.

HALF-AND-HALF METHOD

Step-by-Step

1. Draw a 10-foot ground line to fit the width of the drawing; scale down to find 5 feet and establish the eye line (fig. 7-18).
2. Find line C halfway between the ground line A and eye line B. Line C is 20 feet away from ground line A. The distance from the halfway line C to the ground line A is always equal to the distance from the ground line A to the viewer.
3. Find the halfway line D between line C and eye line B. This line D is double the previous distance or 40 feet from line C.
4. Line E is 80 feet away from line D, and so on. A cross section will further illustrate this method (fig. 7-19).

SQUARE METHOD

This method is used to find depth in 20-foot increments (fig. 7-20).

Step-by-Step

1. Draw a 10-foot ground line, scale down to find 5 feet, and establish the eye line.
2. Draw a 5-foot square (ABCD) between the ground and eye lines, and draw two diagonal lines (AD and CB) to locate point E. According to the previous method, E is the halfway point between the ground and eye lines. Therefore, AE is 20 feet deep, because you are 20 feet from the picture plane.
3. Draw a horizontal line from E, and intersect line AC at F. Connect F to D, intersecting line CB at G. Draw a horizontal line through G, intersecting line AD at I. The distance between E and I is also 20 feet.
4. Continue this method to create additional 20-foot increments.

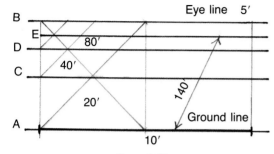

Figure 7-18.

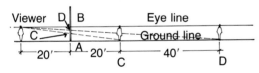

Figure 7-19.

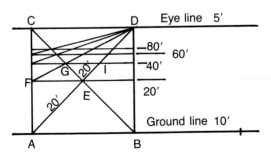

Figure 7-20.

FRACTION METHOD

In figure 7-21, since the viewer is assumed to be 20 feet from the ground line, then any depth needed up from the ground line will be divided by 20. This number is then the numerator. The denominator is the numerator plus 1. This fraction is the portion of the distance between the ground line and the eye line needed to locate the desired depth.

For example, to locate a 60-foot depth: 60 is divided by 20 to equal 3. Then $3/(3 + 1) = \frac{3}{4}$, therefore $\frac{3}{4}$ distance between two lines is 60 feet deep.

The same method applied to 40, 80, 160, and 480 foot depths will result in fractions of $\frac{2}{3}$, $\frac{4}{5}$, $\frac{8}{9}$, and $\frac{24}{25}$. If the viewer is, for example, 10 feet from the ground line, then the distance needed should be divided by 10.

PROPORTIONAL METHOD

This method will find the odd distance such as 7, 14, or $47\frac{3}{4}$ feet. The needed depth from the ground line should always include the distance between the ground line to the viewer, for which 20 feet is assumed. In this example, a 20-, 45-, and 62-foot depth from the ground line are needed.

Step-by-Step

1. Draw the ground line and assume it to be 10 feet long (fig. 7-22). Scale down to find 5 feet and locate the eye line.

2. Place the 0 on the edge of an engineer's scale anywhere on the ground line.

3. Place the desired depth of 40-foot mark (20 plus 20) on the eye line. The 20-foot mark on the scale is the point of the desired depth of 40 feet from the viewer, or 20 feet from the ground line.

4. The same process is used in figure 7-23 to find the depth of 65 feet (45 plus 20). Place 0 on the ground line and 65 on the eye line. The 45-foot mark on the scale is there-

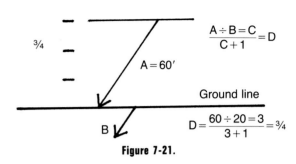

Figure 7-21.

A = Depth needed from ground line

B = Distance from viewer to ground line

C = Numerator

D = Ratio between eye and ground lines on the desired location of the needed depth

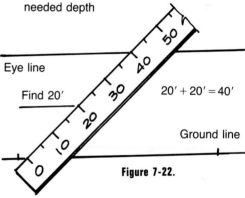

Figure 7-22.

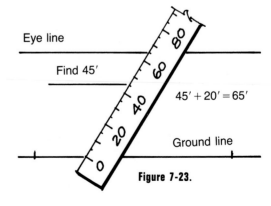

Figure 7-23.

fore the desired depth of 65 feet from the viewer, or 45 feet from the ground line.

5. In order to get a 62-foot depth from the ground line (fig. 7-24), place the 0 on the ground line and 82 (62 plus 20) on the eye line. The 62-foot mark on that scale is the required depth.

6. If the viewer is 10 feet away from the ground line, any needed depth from the ground line should add only 10 feet (instead of 20 feet).

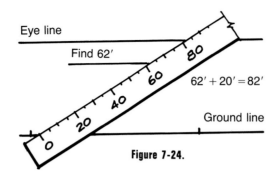

Figure 7-24.

Eye line

Find 62'

$62' + 20' = 82'$

Ground line

CROSS-CHECK ON ALL FOUR METHODS

To cross-check all four methods of finding the same depth in a perspective drawing, we will assume the viewer is 20 feet away from the ground line and the locations of the 20-foot and 60-foot depth on all four methods are exactly the same points. Choose the method most appropriate for the drawing (fig. 7-25).

ONE-POINT PERSPECTIVE

A one-point perspective is created when the viewer is looking at the object in front of him head-on, as opposed to viewing it at an angle. The viewer is directly in front of the vanishing point. If the viewer moves, the vanishing point also moves. One-point perspective is easy to learn and construct, although the result is not as dynamic as two- or three-point perspective. An office method of constructing one-point perspective and a quick method are given below.

OFFICE METHOD

Laying out a one-point perspective using the office method is accurate but time consuming and tedious. Nevertheless, the principles of the office method are the basis for the quick method.

In this example, we will construct a one-point perspective of a courtyard or interior

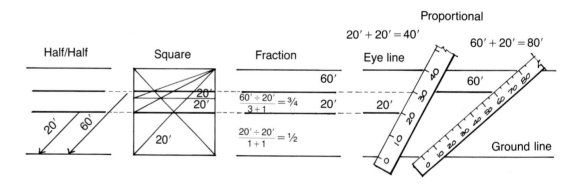

Figure 7-25.

space, 20 feet deep and 20 feet wide, surrounded by a wall that is 10 feet high. There is a box in the courtyard 3½ feet wide, 5 feet long, and 3 feet high. The box is 5 feet from the picture plane, and the viewer is 15 feet away from the picture plane, standing directly in front of the center of the space.

Step-by-Step

1. Draw the picture plane, placing the floor plan on it (fig. 7-26). Locate the station point 15 feet from the picture plane. Use a straightedge and, through the picture plane, connect the station point to points C, D, E, F, G, and H.

2. Draw the ground line at any desired location (fig. 7-27). Establish a 5-foot eye line using the same scale as in the plan. Locate the vanishing point on the eye line by dropping a vertical line from the station point. Where lines from points C, D, E, F, G, and H intersect the picture plane, drop vertical lines to the ground line.

3. Locate the outer edges of the wall W and X. Use any method discussed earlier to find the wall height of 10 feet for points R and S. Connect points W, X, R, and S to the vanishing point to establish the base and top of the walls. Find back wall PQYZ.

4. Place the footprint of the block on the floor plan, and use any of the previous methods to locate height.

QUICK METHOD

The following method illustrates step-by-step how to set up a typical one-point perspective. This unique method also allows you to control the size of the perspective from the beginning and avoid awkwardly sized drawings.

The width of the space generally should not exceed 60 feet if the eye level is 5 feet. The example shown is a courtyard that is 20 feet wide and 20 feet deep, with a 10-foot-high wall. The viewer is standing in the middle, 20 feet outside of the space.

Step-by-Step

1. Draw the ground line toward the bottom of the drawing (fig. 7-28). Allow a 1-to-3-inch white space on the right, left, and bottom edges of the paper.

Divide the ground line in four equal spaces; each one will represent 5 feet.

2. Establish the eye line (horizon line) at 5 feet above the ground line by using an arc or a 45-degree line to transfer a 5-foot increment from the ground line (fig. 7-29).

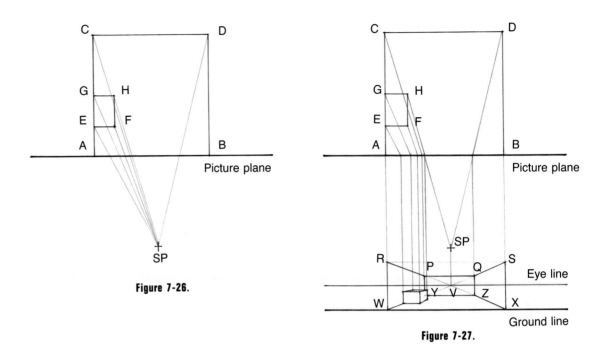

Figure 7-26.

Figure 7-27.

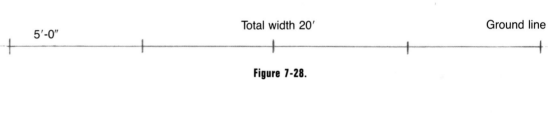

Figure 7-28.

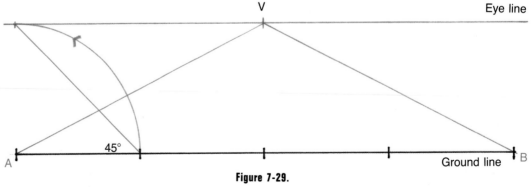

Figure 7-29.

Locate the vanishing point (V) in the center. This means that the viewer is directly in the center of the space but 20 feet outside the space. Connect points A and B to V to establish the two base lines of the space.

3. Find the 20-foot depth by locating C between A and V (fig. 7-30). The distance from A to C is 20 feet. The distance AC is also equal to how far away the viewer is from the ground line (or the picture plane). The back wall should not be too far toward the eye line or too close to the ground line.

To locate D, draw a line parallel to the ground line from point C to intersect line BV.

To locate the height of the back wall of the courtyard (CG and DH), draw two vertical lines from points C and D. Because we assumed a 5-foot eye level, every vertical line dropped from the horizon line to the ground will have a height of 5 feet. Therefore, to locate the height of the wall at 10 feet, we simply double the length of the line from C to the eye line. Draw a horizontal line from G to H to complete the back wall.

4. To complete the front picture plane, draw lines from V to G and V to H, extending them until they are at least directly above A and B. Draw vertical lines upward from A and B. Where they intersect the diagonals are points I and J. To complete the ceiling, connect I and J.

5. Divide the ground line into twenty 1-foot intervals (fig. 7-31). Connect each point to point V. Connect C and B, and where CB intersects each 1-foot interval line, draw horizontal lines to complete the floor grid.

6. Divide the vertical edge of the back wall into ten equal parts and connect each point to point V, extending each line to the edge of the wall.

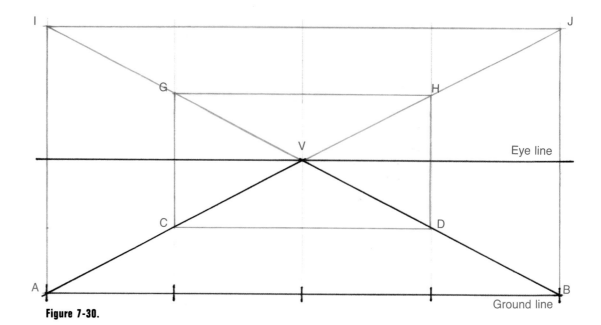

Figure 7-30.

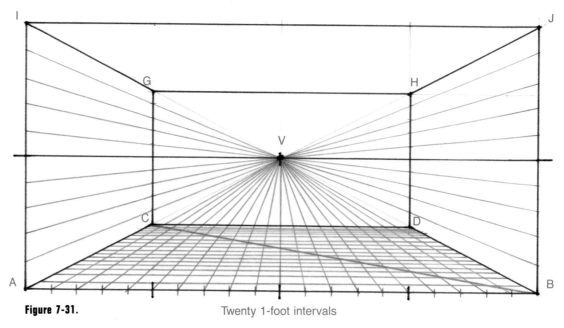

Figure 7-31. Twenty 1-foot intervals

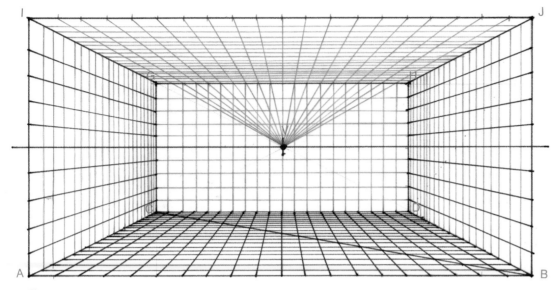

Figure 7-32.

7. Where the horizontal lines of the floor grid meet the base line of the wall, draw vertical lines (fig. 7-32).

8. Draw the ceiling grid using projections from the floor and wall, and complete the side wall and ceiling.

9. Locate the footprint of objects on the floor grid. (In figure 7-33, a person is located.)

Draw vertical lines from the corners of the object up to the horizon line. This will give the object a height of 5 feet.

Adjust the height according to the object. Remember that all vertical lines in the space are drawn vertical in the perspective; horizontal lines are drawn parallel to the horizon line. When all the heights of the objects have been found and drawn, complete the entourage to complete the one-point perspective drawing.

EXAMPLE: Figure 7-34.

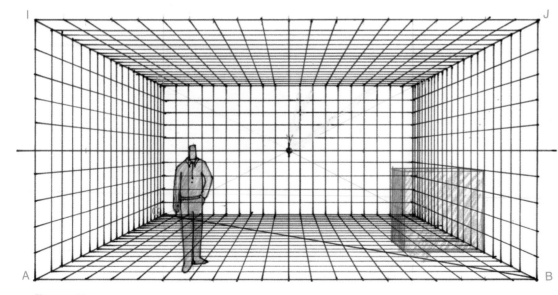

Figure 7-33.

Figure 7-34. Top left: Steve Allenstein; top right: Janet Galloway; bottom right: Peter Williams; bottom left: Brian Lin; participants ML Graphic Workshop. Marker, colored pencil, felt-tip pen, and pastel on 19″ × 24″ marker paper each. 1 hour each including designing time.

Two-Point Perspective

A two-point perspective is a dynamic and useful means of studying three-dimensional objects. It is created when the viewer is looking at an object from an angle. Generally, it is more complex to set up than a one-point perspective, unless you are working on an established grid or chart. Here we will review the office method and introduce an alternative quick method.

OFFICE METHOD

The office method allows you to set up a perspective from any desired angle; all that is required is a plan and elevation of the design project. However, it is time consuming, and the size of the completed perspective is unpredictable. Also, it is hard to locate foreground elements such as cars and street lights. Even if you prefer to use the quick method, or a perspective chart (discussed later in this chapter), the fundamental principles of the office method should be understood; they form the basis for the other methods discussed in this chapter.

In the example, we will construct a two-point perspective of a building which is 20 feet wide by 10 feet deep by 10 feet high. We will be standing 30 feet away from the corner of the building and viewing at a $^{30}\!/_{60}$-degree angle. Steps 1 to 3 in the following step-by-step instructions show establishing a view from above, which includes plan, station point, two vanishing points, and a line representing the picture plane (a "glass" that the viewer sees through and draws on). Steps 4 and 5 introduce eye and ground lines, elevation, and two vanishing points on the eye line. Step 6 illustrates how the two-point perspective is constructed.

Step-by-Step

1. Draw the picture plane, line 1 (fig. 7-35). Place the floor plan of the building on the picture plane at a $^{30}\!/_{60}$-degree angle. This angle will provide an ideal view. Use the same scale as the floor plan, and locate the station point at 30 feet below the corner of the building (since you are standing 30 feet away from the corner).

2. From the station point, draw line 2 parallel to the right side of the building. Where this line intersects the picture plane is the right vanishing point (RVP). Repeat this procedure to locate the left vanishing point (LVP) with line 3.

3. With a straightedge project line 4 from the station point to every corner of the building. Stop where they hit the picture plane (points G, H, and I).

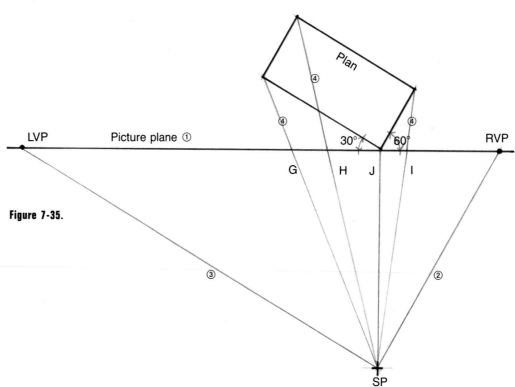

Figure 7-35.

4. Draw the ground line at any desired location (line 5), and place the side elevation of the building on it; elevation and plan should be at the same scale (fig. 7-36).

5. Still using the same scale, draw the eye line (line 6) 5 feet above the ground line. Locate the RVP and the LVP on the eye line by dropping them vertically from the picture plane (lines 7). Project the height of the building from the elevation (line 8) to line 9 and intersect at K.

6. Connect points K and L to RVP and LVP, respectively (lines 10) and drop points G, H, and I vertically (fig. 7-37). These lines (lines 9) will intersect on lines 10 at points A,B,C, and D. Thus the two-point perspective building is completed.

QUICK METHOD

This method is very useful for rough drawings when a perspective chart is not available. The example is a building that is 40 feet long, 20 feet deep, and 25 feet high. The viewer is 5 feet tall, standing at a $^{30}\!/_{60}$-degree angle to the building.

Step-by-Step

1. Draw an eye line to represent the 5-foot level (fig. 7-38). Locate the two vanishing points, on both ends of the eye line (AB). Their placement is arbitrary.

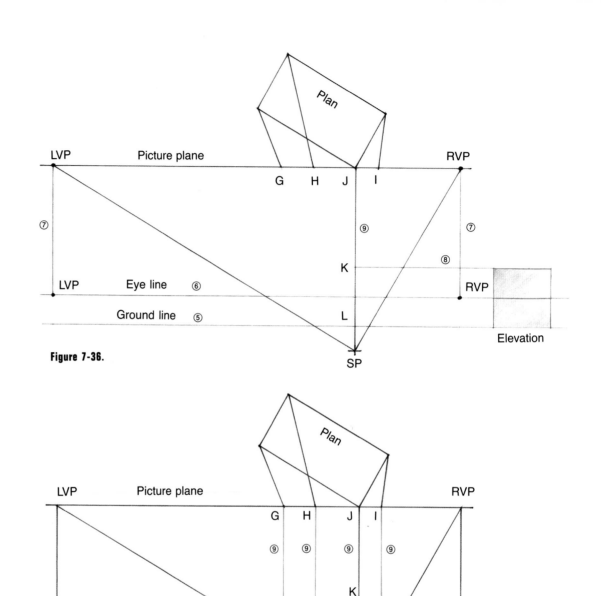

Figure 7-36.

Figure 7-37.

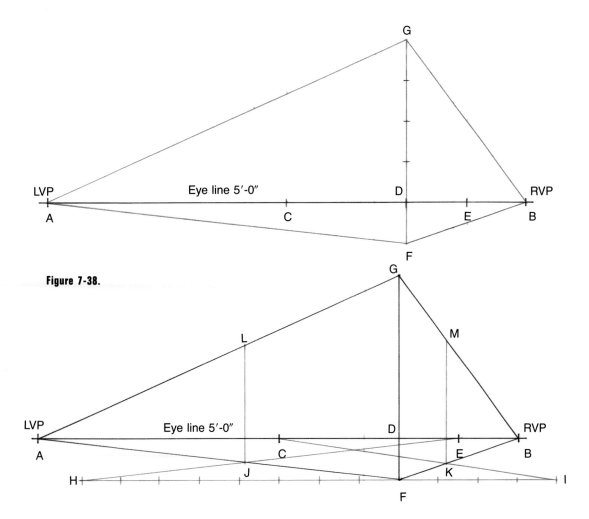

Figure 7-38.

on the building, first locate them on lines HF or FI, and project points on line HF to point E to arrive on line JF. Then project points on line FI to point C to arrive on line FK.

Evenly Spaced Lines: Step-by-Step

1. Draw a building and locate the middle point B, which is half the height of the building (fig. 7-39). Then project a line through B to the left vanishing point (line 2).

2. Connect A to B and extend to intersect with line 1 at point D.

3. Draw vertical line DE down from D, intersecting line 2 at X. The distance AC is equal to CE.

4. Now connect point C to X and extend to line 1 to find point F. Draw a vertical line FG. CE is equal to EG.

5. Repeat this step as needed to find more equal increments.

Notice that lines AD, CF, EH, and so on will eventually intersect at a point that is located directly above the left vanishing point. This fact may be used to check accuracy.

2. Find point C in the middle of the eye line, LVP and RVP, point D in the middle of line CB, and point E in the middle of line DB.

3. Use point D as the corner of the building (line DB is one-fourth of line AB); draw a vertical line. Locate point F as the base; line DF is 5 feet high. Use stacking method to find the 25-foot height of the building (FG). If the building needs to be closer to the viewer, simply lengthen line DF. Connect AG, AF, BG, and BF.

4. From point F, draw a line parallel to the eye line, and using the same scale as at the corner of the building (line DF equals 5 feet), measure 40 feet from F to locate point H, and measure 20 feet from F to locate point I. Connect H to E and intersect line AF at J. Connect I to C and intersect line BF at point K. Draw vertical lines upward from points J and K to find points L and M.

5. The building is now completed. Add details and entourage. To find specific points

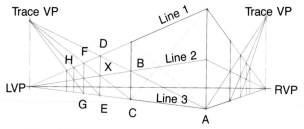

Figure 7-39.

CIRCLE IN PERSPECTIVE

In these two methods, the first is somewhat sketchier and can be used for roughs, while the second, though more complicated, is more precise.

Step-by-Step: Method One

1. Locate a square A,B,C,D in perspective (fig. 7-40).
2. Draw diagonal lines AC and BD; find points E,F,G,H.
3. Find point I, which is a little less than ¾ of line BO (or divide line BO to half and another half but less). Use the same method to obtain points J,K, and L.
4. Freehand, with repeat-line technique, connect E,I,F,J,G,K,H,L to complete the circle.

Step-by-Step: Method Two

1. Locate a square A,B,C,D in perspective and divide lines BC and CD into four increments (fig. 7-41). From the increments, draw 16 equal squares.
2. Connect point A to points H and M; point B to points K and P; point C to points G and N; and point D to points J and E.
3. Freehand, with repeat-line technique, connect points F, O, L, I and other intersecting points. The circle in perspective is completed.

USING PERSPECTIVE CHARTS

An established two-point perspective chart is quick and easy to use. It is especially effective when used with tracing paper.

The chart shown here (fig. 7-42) is based on a ³⁰⁄₆₀-degree perspective with the following givens:
• The viewer is 5 feet tall, standing at a ³⁰⁄₆₀ degree angle against the grid to use the optimum cone of vision.
• The floor and ceiling grid are 50 feet apart and connected by a scaled pole, which is 40 feet from the viewer's right arm, 70 feet from the left arm, and 80 feet from the viewer. Both grids and the viewer are stationary, and the eye line is at 5-foot level.
• The chart is shown on a 1-foot increment; every tenth foot, the line is thicker for easy calculation. X-numbers indicate depth; Y-numbers, width.
• Two dotted horizontal lines represent the picture plane, and the dotted circle indicates the viewer's cone of vision. The elements of the drawing should be kept within this circle to avoid distortion. Both vanishing points are indicated. The perspective chart is made in a set of three sizes to facilitate the drawing dimensions: small (11″×17″), medium (17″×24″), and large (24″×36″). It is

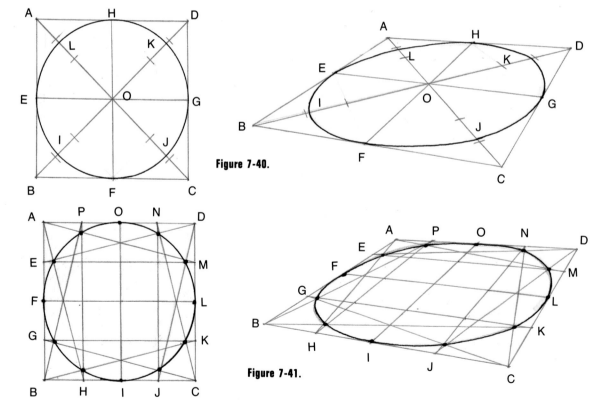

Figure 7-40.

Figure 7-41.

printed on both sides for versatile views and on fine quality plastic paper for durability. These can be obtained through the Mike Lin Graphic Workshop at 2815 Amherst Avenue, Manhattan, Kansas 66502. Tel: (913) 537-2919, 537-1666. Fax: (913) 537-3366.

In the following examples, the chart is used to set up two-point perspectives of a building, multiple buildings, an interior space or courtyard, and an aerial view.

BUILDING

The building in this example (fig. 7-42) is 70 feet wide in the front, 30 feet deep, and 30 feet high. The side of the building is 40 feet away from the viewer's right arm, and the front of the building is 70 feet from the viewer's left arm. There is a 20-foot-wide sidewalk in front of the building, and a 30-foot-wide street adjacent to the sidewalk (see plan view).

Step-by-Step

1. Locate point B at the top of the pole (indicated by 50), at seven 10-foot intervals toward the LVP on line X70 find point A, and at three 10-foot intervals toward the RVP on line Y40 find point C. This forms the 70-by-30-foot floor plan on the 50-foot-high ceiling.

2. Locate point E at the bottom of the pole (indicated by 0); connect it to the RVP and the LVP to locate the base of the building.

3. Project A and C down vertically to the base to form the edge of the building, intersecting the base lines at D and F.

4. Locate the 30-foot mark G on the vertical pole, and connect it to both the RVP and LVP to locate the top of the building. This now completes the outline of the building form.

5. From point E, count two 10-foot intervals outward to position the sidewalk 20 feet

from the building on line X50. Then count three 10-foot intervals outward from the edge of the sidewalk to locate the 30-foot street on line X20.

6. Add details and entourage to complete the perspective.

7. If the right side of the building needs to be shown in greater detail, use the other side of the chart and follow the same process.

Technical Tips

• Because the ceiling grid is established 50 feet above the ground, the viewer is able to perceive depth more easily and accurately. Therefore, locate the floor plan on the ceiling grid and project it down to find the width and depth of the building. The height of the building then can be reduced.

• Remember, a line dropped from the eye line down to any spot on the ground plane is always 5 feet tall.

• The grid can be altered to half or double its size. However, any changes in dimension should apply to all three axes. For example, if the 50-foot-high ceiling becomes 100 feet, the eye line is also doubled to 10 feet, with each 1-foot grid becoming 2 feet.

• Use a red pencil to construct or block out perspective lines. This will allow better readability against the black line on the chart. Red pencil also allows designers to draw more creatively.

MULTIPLE BUILDINGS

In this example (fig. 7-43), the viewer is stationary and the buildings are at various distances. They are indicated in different colors and superimposed on the same chart to show how different buildings can fit into the same cone of vision. Each building is shown in plan and its location from the viewer is given. It will be explained step-by-step how to strategically and propor-

tionately position a building onto the chart. All buildings are the same height (50 feet) yet different sizes; Red Building A is 50 feet wide, 100 feet deep; Green Building B is 40 feet wide, 50 feet deep; Blue Building C is 110 feet wide, 200 feet deep. They can all fit into the viewer's cone of vision.

Step-by-Step: Red Building A

1. On the paper draw the plan of a building that is 50 feet wide in front and 100 feet long on the side. Locate the corner of the plan at point P and draw a line with the front side of the plan at 30 degrees. From point P, draw a perpendicular line.

2. To establish the cone of vision, on the 60-degree corner of a $30/60$-degree triangle, divide the corner in half and draw a split line on the triangle with a pen. Move the triangle so that this line will be parallel to the perpendicular line on the plan. Both edges of the triangle should nearly touch the edge of the building, still allowing a small space on both sides. When this is achieved, mark on the plan along the edges of the triangle; this is the viewer's cone of vision (shown in shaded area).

3. Starting from the corner of the cone of vision (this is where viewer stands) draw two lines, each parallel to the front and side of the building (lines 1 and 2, or viewer's left and right arm).

4. Using the same scale as the plan, measure the distance between the front of the building to line 1, which in this case is 70 feet, and the side of the building to line 2, which is 40 feet.

5. As determined in step 4, the viewer is standing 70 feet from the front of the building and 40 feet from the side of the building. Because this is within the cone of vision, the building will be viewed properly. On the ceiling grid, count inward from the left arm

X0 for seven 10-foot intervals (X70), and from the right arm Y0 for four 10-foot intervals (Y40). When line X70 and Y40 intersect, the top of the corner of the building (A1) is found.

6. Since point A1 coincides with the top of the scaled pole, and the building is 50 feet tall, the base of the building A2 will coincide with 0.

7. From point A1, count five 10-foot intervals toward the LVP to find point A3, and ten 10-foot intervals toward the RVP to find point A4. This will establish the top edges of the building.

8. Connect A2 to the RVP and the LVP to locate the base of the building.

9. From points A3 and A4, project vertical lines down to intersect the base at points A5 and A6, thus completing the shape of the building.

Step-by-Step: Green Building B

The green building B is 40 feet wide in the front, 50 feet deep, and 50 feet high. Since this building is smaller in size, it needs to be brought forward toward the viewer in order to fit the cone of vision correctly. Basically follow the same steps as building A.

1. On the paper, draw the plan of the building, which is 40 feet wide in the front and 50 feet deep along the side.

2. Locate the corner of the plan at point Q, and draw a line with the front side of the building plan at 30 degrees.

3. From point Q, draw a perpendicular line down.

4. Again use the 60-degree corner of the triangle, keeping the line marked on the triangle parallel to the perpendicular line of the plan. Frame the plan as discussed in the red building. Mark on the plan along the edges of the triangle to form the cone of vision.

5. From the corner of the cone of vision, project two lines 3 and 4, each parallel to the front and side of the building plan.

6. Using the same scale as the plan, measure the distance between the front of the building to line 3, which is 50 feet, and the side of the building to line 4, which is 20 feet.

7. On the ceiling grid, count inward from X0 for five 10-foot intervals to find line X50, and from Y0 for two 10-foot intervals to find line Y20. When lines X50 and Y20 intersect, the top of the corner of the building, point B1, is found.

8. Use the height-projection method explained under one-point perspective to find the base of the building. First connect point B1 to A1 on the red building and extend to the horizon line to obtain point M (this happens to coincide with a point marked 45 VP). From point M, extend a line through point A2 on the red building and intersect at B2 with the vertical line drawn from point B1.

9. From point B1, count four 10-foot intervals toward the LVP to find point B3, and five 10-foot intervals toward the RVP to find point B4.

10. Connect B2 to RVP and the LVP to locate the base of the green building B.

11. Draw vertical lines from points B3 and B4 to intersect with the base lines. This will complete the shape of the 50-foot tall green building.

Step-by-Step: Blue Building C

The blue building C is 110 feet wide in the front, 200 feet deep, and 50 feet high. However, since it is four times larger than the red building A, it needs to be pushed further away from the viewer, in order to fit in the cone of vision.

1. On the paper, draw the plan of building, which is 110 feet wide in the front, 200 feet along the side.

2. Locate the corner of the plan point R, and draw a line with the front side of the building plan at 30 degrees.

3. From point R, draw a perpendicular line down.

4. Use the 60-degree corner of the triangle, and frame the building on the plan to form the cone of vision.

5. From the corner of the cone of vision, project two lines 5 and 6. Each shall be parallel to the front and side of the building plan.

6. Using the same scale as the plan, measure the distance between the front of the building to line 5, which is 120 feet, and side of the building to line 6, which is 60 feet.

7. On the ceiling grid, count inward from X0 for twelve 10-foot intervals to find line X120, and from Y0 for six 10-foot intervals to find line Y60. When lines X120 and Y60 intersect, the top corner of the building (C1) is found.

8. Using a straightedge, connect points A1 to C1 and extend to the eye line to find point N. Connect point N with A2 on the red building. This will intersect at C2 with the vertical line drawn from point C1.

9. From point C1, count eleven 10-foot intervals toward the LVP to find point C3, and twenty 10-foot intervals toward the RVP to find point C4.

10. Connect C2 to RVP and the LVP to locate the base of the blue building C.

11. Draw vertical lines from points C3 and C4 to intersect with the base lines, thus completing the shape of the 50-foot-tall blue building C.

After the above three exercises, it is apparent that three different sized buildings can all be controlled and shown within the

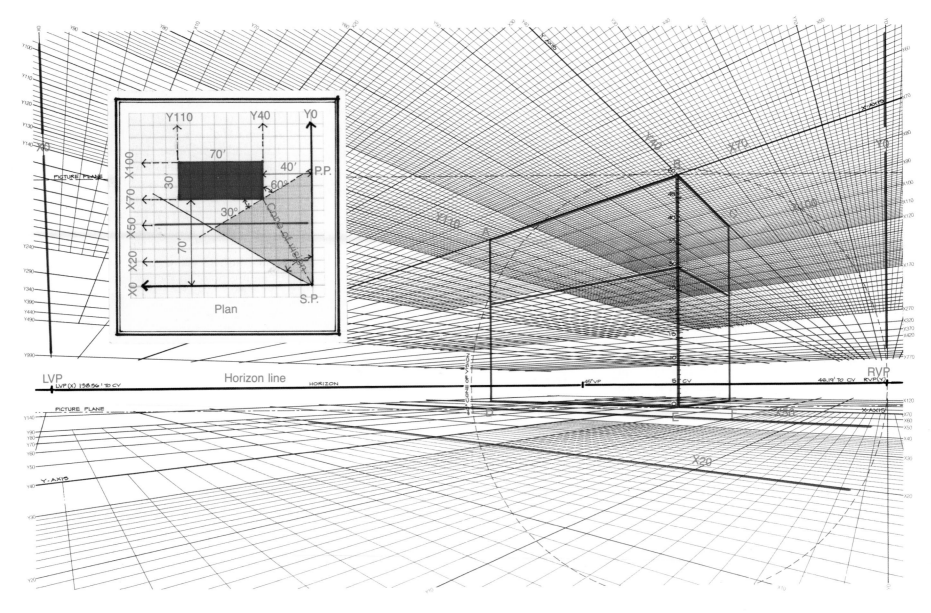

Figure 7-42.

viewer's cone of vision as indicated in the dotted circle on the chart. The biggest, the blue building, the furthest way from the viewer, appears to be shorter, while the smallest, the green building, the closest to the viewer, appears to be taller, but in fact, they are all the same height—50 feet tall.

Having understood the method discussed above, any building with a plan fitting inside within a 60-degree triangle can easily be constructed on one of the three sizes of the perspective chart to meet the desired size of the presentation drawings. A designer can then revise or recreate the design easily in a three dimensional manner.

EXAMPLE: Figure 7-44 is an example of a two-point perspective constructed using the above method.

INTERIOR SPACE OR COURTYARD

This courtyard or interior space (fig. 7-45) is 30 feet wide, 20 feet deep, and 10 feet high. The viewer is 5 feet tall and standing along the right side of the space and 10 feet away from the front at a $^{30}/_{60}$-degree angle.

Step-by-Step

1. Draw the base of the right wall line Y0. Count 30 feet toward the left to find line AC (line Y30).
2. Draw the base of the front space (line X10). Count 20 feet to the back to find line CF (line X30). Lines Y30 and X30 intersect at point C.
3. From C, draw a vertical line up to establish a 10-foot-high ceiling at point D (use stacking method).
4. From D, following the grid, find DG to complete the top of the back wall. Also from D and following the grid, find DB to com-

plete the top of the left wall. Connect A and B. To finish the ceiling, connect B and E.
5. Include details and entourage in the space by locating their footprints on the floor grid and projecting them upward.

Technical Tips

• When drawing a courtyard or an interior space, remember that the viewer is very close to the space.
• Start with line Y0 as the right edge of the space and count the width of the space to the left. Use line X10 as the front of the space and count the depth toward the back.
• Always locate the footprint of elements of design on the floor grid first and establish their height accordingly.

EXAMPLE: Figure 7-46.

AERIAL VIEW

An aerial perspective is used mainly in large, complex projects to provide an over-all view of the entire scheme. It is also called a bird's-eye view. The same chart is used but it is turned upside down.

The building in the example is 50 feet in front, 50 feet on the side, and 30 feet tall (fig. 7-47). Locate the building 40 feet from the viewer's left arm and 70 feet from the right arm.

Step-by-Step

1. From the left arm (Y0) on the grid, count four 10-foot intervals, and draw line Y40. From the right arm (X0) on the grid, count inward seven 10-foot intervals, and draw line X70 intersecting with the previous drawn line to find point A.
2. From point A, count five 10-foot intervals toward the LVP to find point C, and five 10-foot intervals toward the RVP to find point D. This creates the base of the building.

3. Since point A coincides with the bottom of the scaled pole, count 30 feet up from point A to find point B and establish the height of the building. Draw vertical lines up from points C and D. From point B, follow the grid lines, draw lines toward RVP and LVP and intersect at points F and E with the vertical lines previously drawn to establish the top of the building.
4. From point E, draw a line toward the RVP, and from point F, draw a line toward the LVP. The two lines will intersect at point G to complete the shape of the building.
5. Add details and entourage. Remember that the eye line is now 45 feet. Therefore, a 5-foot person at any spot on the ground plane should be scaled down accordingly (one-ninth of the distance of the person's standing point to the eye line).

Technical Tips

The eye line is at 45 feet. Because the grid is now flipped upside down, the ceiling and floor grid are 50 feet apart. With the eye line at 45 feet, a line drawn down from the horizon line to anywhere on the ground line is 45 feet high ($50 - 5 = 45$).

Always locate the floor plan of the building or layout of the site plan on the ground plane, because with the chart upside down the floor grid is more easily read than the ceiling grid.

EXAMPLE: Figure 7-48.

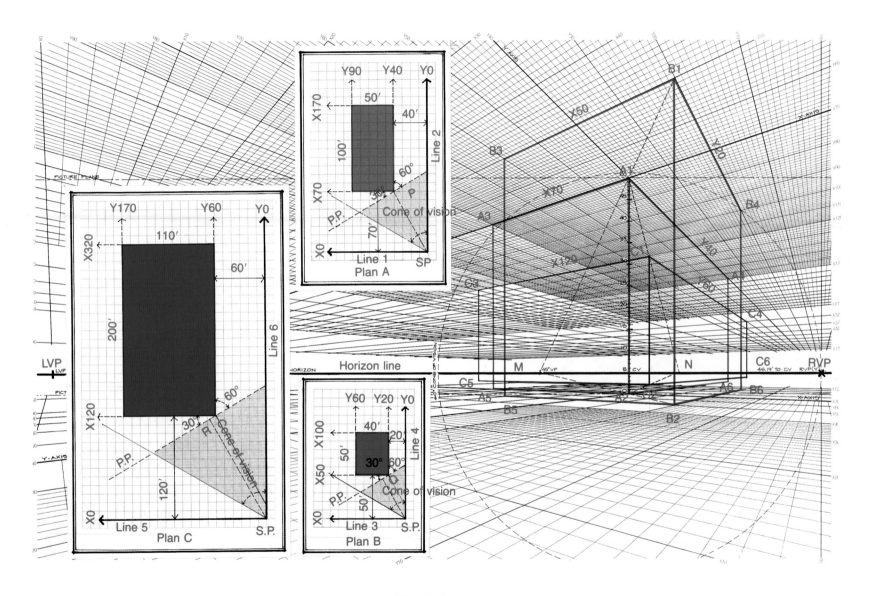

Figure 7-43.

Figure 7-44. Top left: Sherman Shook; top right: Steve Allenstein; bottom left: Eric Sweet; bottom right: Janet Galloway; participants, ML Graphic Workshop. Marker, colored pencil, and felt-tip pen on 19″ × 24″ marker paper each. 1 to 2½ hours each including designing time.

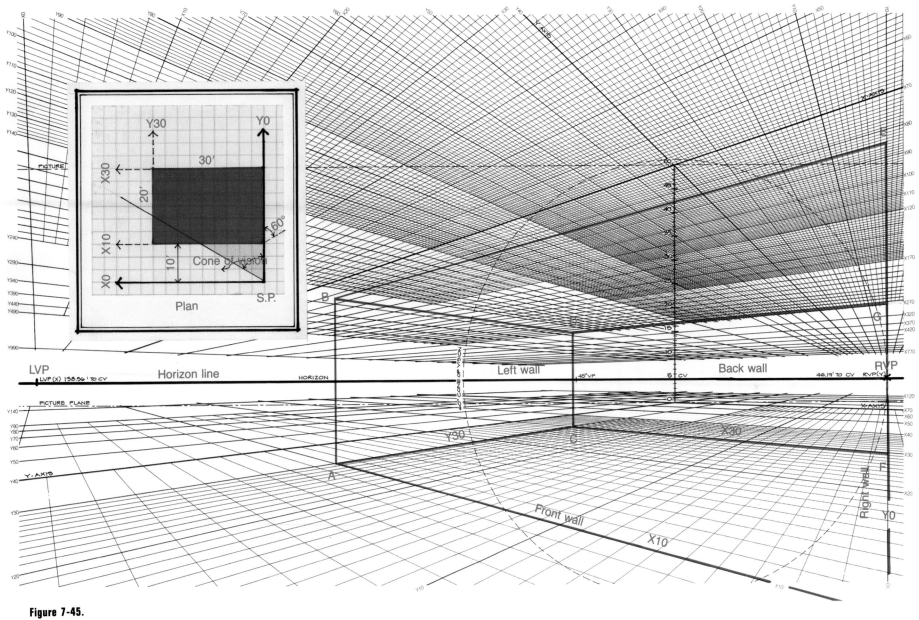

Figure 7-45.

Figure 7-46. Top left: Peter Williams; top right: Steve Allenstein; bottom left: Travis Rice; bottom right: Annemarie Kaune; participants, ML Graphic Workshop. Marker, colored pencil, and felt-tip pen on 19″ × 24″ marker paper each. 1 to 2 hours each including designing time.

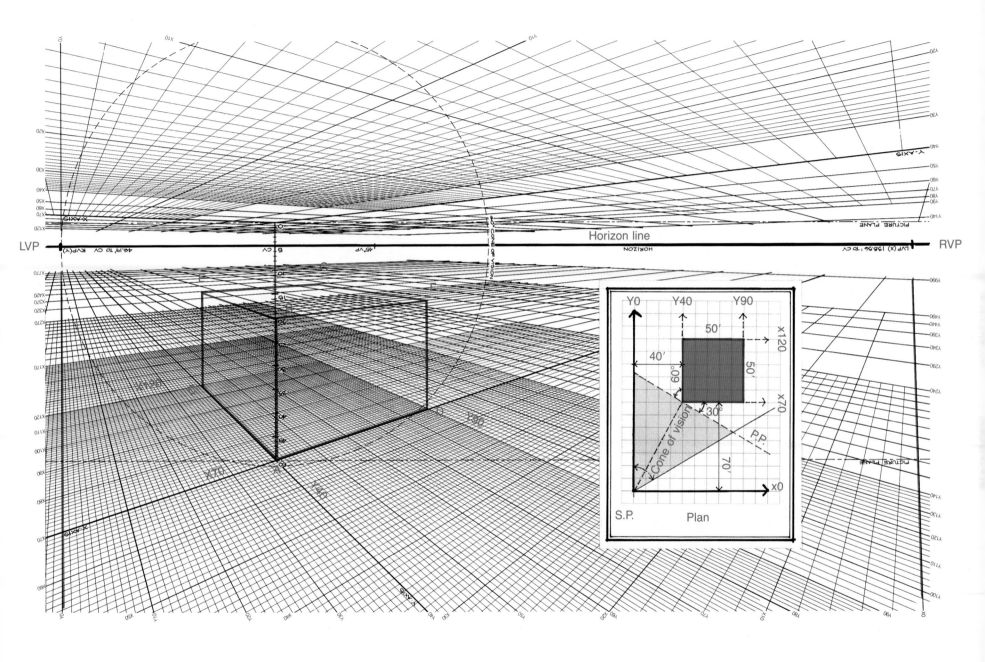

Horizon line

LVP

RVP

Y0 Y40 Y90

50'

40'

60°

50'

30°

70'

Cone of vision

P.P.

x120

x70

x0

S.P.

Plan

Figure 7-47.

Figure 7-48. Top left: Shelley Stephenson; top right: Steven Savonen; bottom left: Bethany Goff; bottom right: Darren Reno; participants, ML Graphic Workshop. Marker, colored pencil, felt-tip pen, and pastel on 19″ × 24″ marker paper each. 3 to 5 hours each including designing time.

PARALINE DRAWING TECHNIQUE

Using a paraline drawing, also known as an axonometric projection, is a fast and easy way to construct a perspective-like drawing and show overall space relationships. It is like showing a floor plan in three dimensions. To use this method, have a floor plan and elevation at hand (fig. 7-49).

Step-by-Step

1. Tape the plan down on the desk so that you are looking at it from the same viewing angle that you want in the final drawing (fig. 7-50).

2. Draw the view line, a long arrow that points in the direction the viewer is looking.

3. Mark a point on the view line "anywhere," but near the bottom is the best place. This is the viewer's-level point.

4. Draw a tickline (fig. 7-51) by placing a piece of tracing paper over the elevation and drawing a line perpendicular to the ground line. Mark or tick the line at each change in the horizontal level of a plane. Label each level.

5. Align the tickline and view line (fig. 7-52) by positioning the tickline over the view line with the top tick on the viewer-level point.

6. Draw one level at a time. Draw the top level, then move the tickline parallel to the view line to align the second tick mark with the viewer's level point. Draw the middle level and connect vertical lines to complete the vertical planes.

7. Repeat step 6 for each level. Move to the next tick mark, repeat step 6 for bottom level, and complete the drawing. An example using this technique is shown in Figure 7-53.

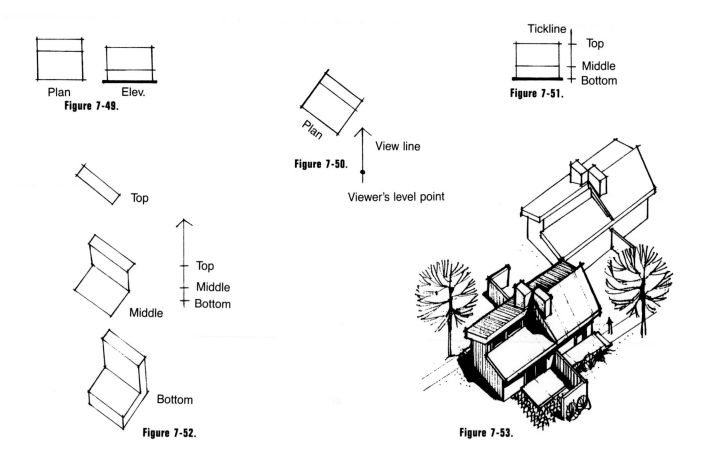

Plan   Elev.
Figure 7-49.

Plan
Figure 7-50.

View line

Viewer's level point

Tickline
Top
Middle
Bottom
Figure 7-51.

Top

Top
Middle
Bottom

Middle

Bottom

Figure 7-52.

Figure 7-53.

PERSPECTIVE TRANSFERRING METHODS

The quickest and easiest way to create a perspective drawing is to use one of the following transfer methods. This can help to avoid laying out perspectives or sketches mechanically and will save time and increase productivity.

ACETATE TRACING
Step-by-Step: From Floor/Site Plan
1. Place the floor/site plan on a table at a desirable angle and add a vertical element (such as a felt-tip marker or an architect's scale that will stand on the table) as a reference to establish the height. Make sure that the height of this vertical element corresponds to the scale of the plan.
2. Tape a sheet of acetate over a plexiglass (or frame a piece of acetate between two windows of cardboard). Hold the acetate in front of you in a vertical position.
3. Draw what you see on the acetate with a felt-tip pen, and create a rough sketch of the plan. (Make sure the vertical element is included to establish height.)
4. On a drafting table, place tracing paper over the acetate and locate the vanishing points and the horizon line. (If it is a two-point perspective, make sure the two vanishing points are on the horizon line.)
5. Add details.

Step-by-Step: From Existing Space
1. Repeat step 2 of the previous method.
2. Stand in front of the existing space at the desired angle and hold the acetate in front of you.
3. Draw what you see on the acetate with a felt-tip pen.
4. Locate the vanishing point and horizon line.

5. Add details.
6. In extreme weather conditions, when it is too hot, too cold, or raining, etc., one can place an acetate on the inside of the car window and draw comfortably in a temperature controlled interior.

SLIDE PROJECTING
Step-by-Step: From Floor/Site Plan
1. Place the plan on the table with a vertical element (as discussed in previous method).
2. Take a 35 mm picture at a desired angle and develop film as a slide.
3. Project the slide onto the wall and trace the image on paper. If possible, place the projector with the slide image reversed on the other side of a glass door, and trace onto tracing paper located on your side of the door. This way, your hand and body will not be in the way.
4. Locate the vanishing point and horizon line.
5. Add details.

Step-by-Step: From Existing Space
1. Take a 35 mm photograph of the existing space at the desired angle.
2. Develop the slide and project it onto a wall and trace the image on desired paper.
3. Locate the vanishing point and horizon line.
4. Add details.
5. Many professionals have used this method to create a proposed design solution from an existing site and present the before and after views to the client (fig. 7-54).

VIDEO CAMERA RECORDING
Step-by-Step: From Floor/Site Plan
1. Place the plan on the table with a vertical element (as discussed in previous method).

2. Use a video camera or camcorder and move around to record it with desired angle.
3. Playback the image on the television screen, and pause at the desired image (unless this view is recorded continuously).
4. Place an acetate over the screen and trace the image quickly.
5. Locate the vanishing point and horizon line.
6. Add details.

Step-by-Step: From Existing Space
1. Use a video camera or camcorder and record the existing space.
2. Follow steps 3 to 6 from above method.

POLAROID ENLARGING
1. Use a polaroid camera to take a picture of the plan or existing space.
2. Enlarge the polaroid picture to the desired size and transfer it to paper.
3. Add details.
4. This process can also be done from any other kind of photo print.

PRINT PAPER DEVELOPING
1. Take a slide at the desired angle of the existing space.
2. In a dark room, project the slide onto undeveloped print paper on the wall.
3. Allow the print paper to be exposed for 30 minutes to several hours, depending on the distance from the projector to the print paper.
4. Use a flashlight occasionally to check the print paper. The process is completed when you notice a distinct yellow and white color on the paper. Immediately run the exposed print paper only through the 'ammonia' process of the blueprint machine. You should now have a view of an existing space on a blue, black, or brownline print paper.

Figure 7-54. Eric Hyne, Land Design/Research, Inc., Columbia, MD. Marker, colored pencil, and tempera on 14″ × 20″ blackline diazo print paper each (original, pen and ink on vellum). 30 hours each.

5. You can use this method to show an existing space, and compare it to a revised design, or other purposes (fig. 7-55).

HOW TO TRANSFER AN IMAGE FROM A DRAWING TO ANOTHER PAPER
Tracing Methods
• Use a light table.
• Use a television screen as a light table with the cable signal disconnected and the volume turned off.
• Use a window or glass door as a light table and trace accordingly.

Transfer Methods
• Place a graphite paper between the original and presentation paper or shade the back of the original drawing using pencil lead powder (and a tissue) or a 6B (soft) pencil. Trace lines accordingly.
• Place tracing paper over the original drawing and use a ball point pen to trace. This is to ensure that no lines are missed while tracing. It will also produce another line drawing of the original, for other use.

A   60 min

B   30 min

C   15 min

Figure 7-55. Images on diazo blueline print paper after 15, 30, and 60 minutes of different exposures from slide projector. The longer the exposure, the lighter the image will be.

8. 永 HOW TO SKETCH

Sketching allows a designer to record an idea quickly, visualize a design, and solve problems as they occur.

Sketching, a spontaneous, freehand activity, incorporates many of the forty-five principles of good graphics: continuous line, zig-zag, white space, focal point, and many others. Understanding and applying these principles will improve your sketching ability. Remember that you can only develop your skills by constant practice. Don't give up.

SKETCHING EXERCISES

To sketch well, you should understand the basic principles of perspective (chapter 7) and should spend some time practicing the forty-five principles of good graphics (chapter 2). Choosing the appropriate medium also makes a difference. A horizontal image, for example, demands a horizontal sheet of paper. Every sketch should at least begin with a pencil-drawn rough layout, without erasures if at all possible. To simplify composition, divide the sheet of paper into three equal parts, horizontally and vertically, to help you locate the objects you are sketching (fig. 8-1). This is known as the rule of thirds. Another preliminary is to make a small frame of stiff paper—8 × 10 inch cardboard or a 3 × 5 inch index card with the center cut out (see fig. 8-2)—to use as a viewfinder and measure perspective angles or porportional space. Be sure to allow sufficient white space. And be sure to include entourage, from people to trees, to clouds, for a lifelike drawing.

The following exercises will help improve your sketching skills:

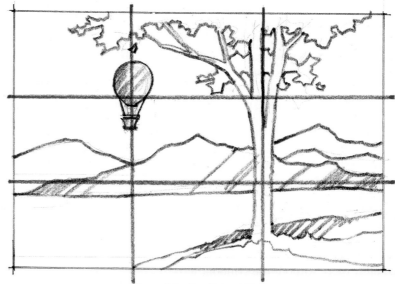

Figure 8-1. The Rule of Thirds.

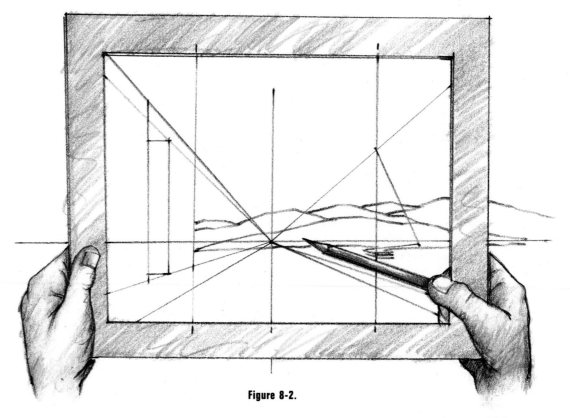

Figure 8-2.

DRAW WITH BOTH HANDS: Draw two different objects at the same time using both hands. In the same sketch, for example, try to draw a tree with your left hand and a building with your right hand. This helps to stimulate right-brain activity.

POSITIVE/NEGATIVE: Observe the shapes and proportions of the entire scene, without worrying about minute details. Try drawing just the negative spaces.

DRAWING UPSIDE DOWN: By drawing an object upside down, you are forced to concentrate on the form in an unconventional manner. This allows you to see and draw what is immediately there without the symbolic left brain's memory of the way the object should look.

DRAW FROM MEMORY: Picture in your mind a familiar object or place you know and draw it. Or look at an image on a slide for a few moments, then turn the projector off, and draw what you have just seen from memory.

TRACING IMAGE FROM SLIDES: Place tracing paper on the wall and quickly trace an image projected from a slide projector. Include the important elements and eliminate unnecessary details.

SKETCH FROM OUT-OF-FOCUS SLIDES: Use pastel and sketch the image from a slide projected that is completely out of focus in the beginning. Every five minutes, sharpen the focus while adding tone to the drawing. In less than half an hour you will see the image drawn in better proportion. Use only the edge of the pastel stick and avoid using hard lines as much as possible.

AN APPROACH TO SKETCHING
Once you have settled on a subject, choose the best angle from which to sketch. Study

the object or scene and envision it on the blank page before you start to work. You will be depicting a three-dimensional subject in two-dimensions on your page and therefore it can be very helpful to view the scene as though you were about to photograph it. Use a paper viewfinder to frame your subject (fig. 8-2). If necessary, apply the rule of thirds and lightly draw three lines vertically and horizontally. Finally, before you begin, review the forty-five principles of good graphics in chapter 2. In the guidelines below, the sketch is based on one-point perspective. Follow the same process for two-point perspective.

Step-by-Step
1. Draw a 5-foot eye line and locate a vanishing point to assist in constructing the perspective and identifying heights of figures. (Remember that if the eye line is at 5 feet, all figures or objects dropped from the eye line will be 5 feet tall.) Draw lines radiating from the vanishing point (fig. 8-3).
2. Rough in the sketch, concentrating on the composition and how it relates to the page. Place the pencil in the cut-out square of the viewfinder to help obtain angles and sizes of objects (see fig. 8-2).
3. Rough in forms in the background, middleground, and foreground. Add the appro-

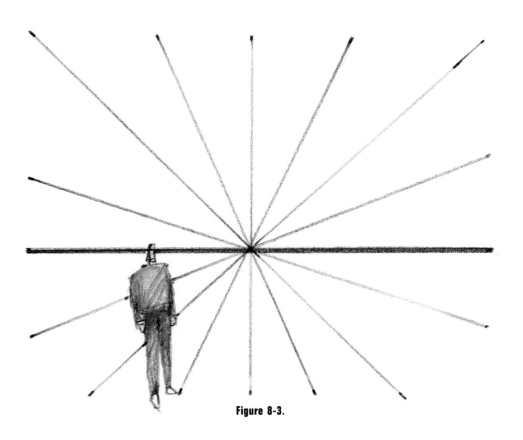

Figure 8-3.

priate entourage such as cars, figures, vegetation, and furniture (fig. 8-4).

4. Develop appropriate values including shade and shadows. Generally, the background will be the lightest, while the foreground should contain the darkest elements. Complete the sketch by adding details where necessary (fig. 8-5).

5. Jot down the location, date, and length of time it took to complete the sketch. This will help you chart your progress by giving you bases for future comparisons.

KEEPING A JOURNAL

Keeping a sketchbook-journal is an excellent way to practice and preserve your sketches. You can also see the progress you make from the first sketches to more sophisticated ones. It will also help you to sketch better through repeated efforts. You can copy thoughts, remember ideas, document your activities for the day, take notes, and practice new lettering styles. A graphic journal needs to be loose, eye-catching, and creative.

Following are some ideas for keeping a graphic journal:

• Make this journal different from an ordinary sketchbook. Use a variety of media: pencil, colored pencil, felt-tip pen, pastel, art stix, and watercolor.
• On an inside cover or on the last page of the book, jot down the forty-five principles of good graphics for handy reference.
• Paste special items in the journal from clippings out of magazines, flyers, newspapers, and so on.
• Add words, phrases, and ideas, and illustrate them with good graphics and colors.

EXAMPLES: Study the journal sketches in figure 8-6, as well as the other drawings (figs. 8-7 to 8-12).

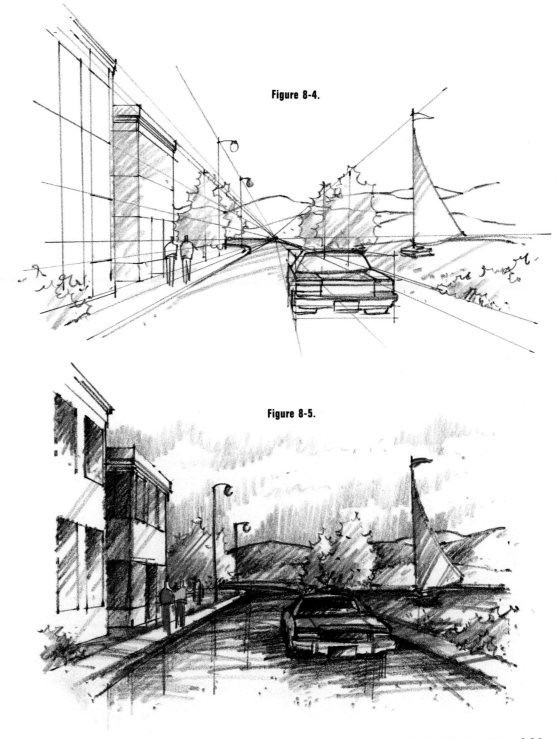

Figure 8-4.

Figure 8-5.

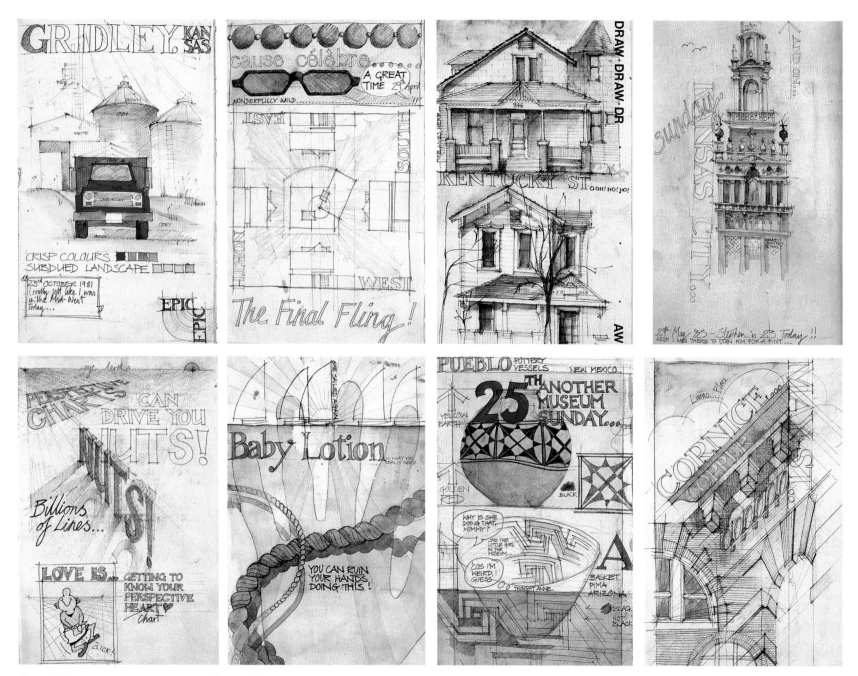

Figure 8-6. Anne Hunt Patterson, Kansas City, MO. Pencil, colored pencil, pen and ink, and watercolor on 5″ × 8″ sketch book. 20 minutes to 1½ hour each.

TOWER BRIDGE 7·31·88

Figure 8-7. Left: Chaturong Chaisupranond, Lockwood Greene Engineers, Inc., Spartanburg, SC. Pen and ink on 8½″ × 11″ vellum; 1 hour each. Right: Rod Henmi, professor, Washington University. Pen and ink on 5″ × 8″ sketch paper. 30 minutes.

Aromandies/Normady '5/90

Aromandies/Normady '5/90

Hydra 3/90

Sandbanks Peninsula/North Haven

Figure 8-8. Paul Laseau, professor, Ball State University. Pen and ink and watercolor on 6″ × 8″ bond paper each. 1 hour each.

Figure 8-9. Left: Kingsley Wu, professor, Purdue University. Marker and felt-tip pen on 8½″ × 11″ marker paper. Top right: Robert S. Oliver, Phoenix, AZ. Felt-tip pen and colored pencil on 6″ × 8″ bond paper. 1 hour. Bottom right: Scott N. Collard, professor, Ball State University. Colored pencil and felt-tip pen on 8½″ × 11″ bond paper. 1 hour.

Figure 8-10. Carl Johnson, Johnson & Roy Inc, Ann Arbor, MI. Watercolor on 5″ × 8″ watercolor paper each. 30 minutes to 1½ hours each.

RUE DE LA HARPE,
PARIS, FRANCE '81

JAISALMER RAJASTHAN
INDIA 1989

MINE 1 GM   MS. SCHEDEN-ANNA

GERMANY

Figure 8-11. Robert S. Oliver, Phoenix, AZ. Felt-tip pen and watercolor on 4″ × 5″ to 6″ × 10″ watercolor paper each. 30 minutes each.

Figure 8-12. Robert S. Oliver, Phoenix, AZ. Felt-tip pen and watercolor on 8″ × 10″ watercolor paper. 30 minutes.

9. 永 DESIGN PROCESS

The design disciplines are varied, but all share the challenge of creating a pleasing design. A successful design is the result of a series of steps known as the design process. This process, in logical sequence, includes establishing the program, setting up bubble diagrams, conducting a site analysis, developing design concepts, generating design approaches, and finally presenting design solutions to the client.

Whether you are an architect, landscape architect, interior designer, urban or regional planner, or graphic designer, you should first establish a program based on certain givens. Client needs, budgets, regulations, surveys and objectives must all be addressed. Based on these criteria, you can develop bubble diagrams. A bubble diagram is a graphic version of an outline. The bubble diagram in figure 9-1 gives an overview of this chapter. In architectural and other projects, it is used to show building spaces, circulatory patterns, and spatial relationships.

While you develop bubble diagrams, you can start conducting a site analysis, taking inventories of views, circulations, climates, topography, vegetation, utilities, and other data according to the nature of the project. Based on the relationships in the bubble diagram and the site analysis, a preliminary design concept can be established. This concept comes through analysis, diagnosis, and synthesis. Its content includes concept diagrams, character sketches, and concept statements. Revisions, based on client feedback, will most likely occur at this stage.

Once the design concept is formulated, and after careful study of the project and the client's responses, the designer can de-

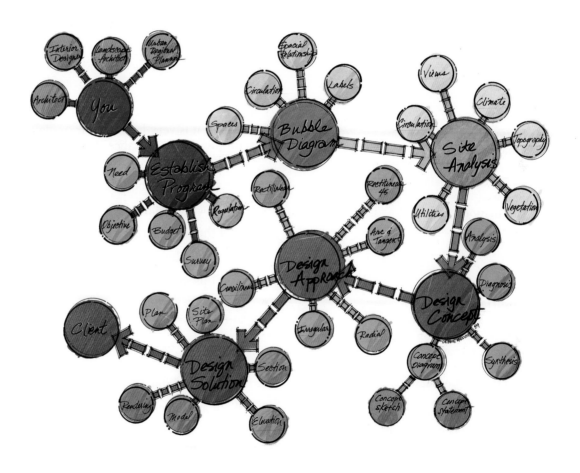

Figure 9-1. A diagram representing the overall relationship of the design process.

termine which design approach is most suitable: rectilinear, rectilinear-45, radial, arc and tangent, irregular, and curvilinear. After choosing the most suitable design approach, the designer can put together design solutions for presentation to the client. This solution includes plans, elevations, sections, details, renderings, and models. A list of the steps in the design process that are discussed in depth in this chapter follows.

THE DESIGN PROCESS
Establish a Program
1. Needs
2. Budgets
3. Regulations
4. Surveys
5. Objectives

Set Up Bubble Diagrams
1. Spaces
2. Circulations
3. Special relationships
4. Labels

Conduct a Site Analysis
1. Subsurface features
2. Natural surface features
3. Cultural and man-made features
4. Aesthetic factors

Develop Design Concepts
1. Processes: analysis, diagnosis, synthesis
2. Products: concept diagrams, character sketches, concept statements

Choose a Design Approach
1. Rectilinear
2. Rectilinear-45
3. Radial
4. Arc-and-tangent
5. Irregular
6. Curvilinear

Present Design Solutions
1. Plans or site plans
2. Elevations
3. Sections
4. Renderings
5. Models

ESTABLISH A PROGRAM

The first step in the design process is to establish the client's needs, budgets, and objectives, and to research local regulations. Some of this can be done by a questionnaire survey. Even if this is done in an interview, however, it is very helpful to formulate all your questions in advance. A few examples of questions are:

What is the total budget for this project?

Will there be stages of development?

Will the site be accessible? to whom?

What will the site be used for?

Will this site be public or private space?

How many people will be using this space at the same time?

How much money is available for landscaping alone?

Is the site visible to and from traffic?

What are the circulation patterns like?

It is also necessary to understand building codes, zoning, and various regulations. These may become limiting factors to your project. For example, is the site zoned for commercial development? Are local building codes compatible with the client's objectives? The kinds of questions will vary according to the client's project and the location.

SET UP BUBBLE DIAGRAMS

Bubble diagrams use bubbles (circles), arrows, and words to represent activities, relationships, and spaces. In the design process, they provide a quick and easy method to study circulation, determine the feasibility of a scheme, present a concept, and achieve a better design.

Step-by-Step
1. Use a red pencil and circle template to draw different size circles which represent the scale and/or importance of the spaces. A good zig-zag layout adds interest to the overall composition. Assign a color to each space (fig. 9-2). This adds excitement and clarity. Use color pair and gradual value change.
2. With a bold Sharpie outline the colored areas first (with overlap corners). Outline again with a felt-tip pen, leaving ⅛-to-1⁄16-inch distance between the two lines (fig. 9-3).
3. Label each bubble with a distinctive bold script lettering. Add stripes and dots with markers, colored pencil, etc. (fig. 9-4).

EXAMPLE: Figure 9-5.

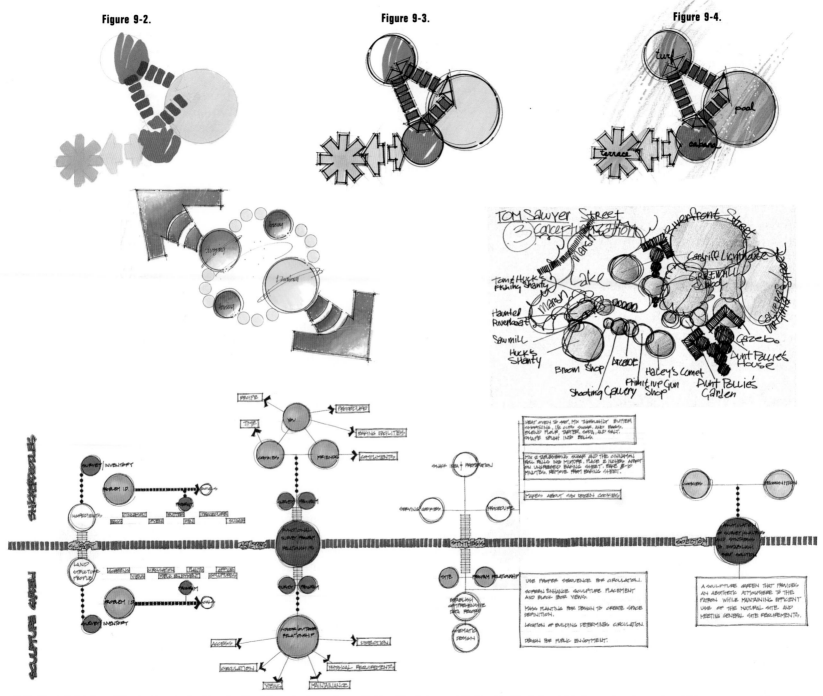

Figure 9-2.

Figure 9-3.

Figure 9-4.

Figure 9-5. Top left: Melissa Woodard; top right: Douglas Saulsbury; bottom: James Dullea. (Participants, ML Graphic Workshop.) Marker, colored pencil, and felt-tip pen on marker, yellow tracing and blackline diazo print paper. 20 minutes to 3 hours each.

Conduct a Site Analysis

Site analysis can be done in conjunction with bubble diagrams. In order to achieve a successful design, site analysis must be done carefully. Missing information may stall the design process as well as increase the construction costs.

Site analysis involves taking an inventory of site elements and analyzing these factors relative to the client's needs and aims. During the inventory stage, you gather all relevant information about the properties of the site, from topography to climate to wind patterns and wildlife. After all such information has been gathered, analyze these features and incorporate them into the design.

If, for example, under topography in the inventory, you discover an area with a 0–5-degree slope, your analysis might be that this is the ideal location for the building. A high spot might have a good view in one direction that can be incorporated into the plan, and a low spot might be right for an artificial lake. Or if there are prevailing northwest winds, you might want to suggest an evergreen screen to act as a buffer. You will also inventory all the existing trees and other plants, and in your analysis make recommendations for those to keep and those to remove.

To help you in compiling your inventory, the following checklist includes many typical considerations.

INVENTORY CHECKLIST
Subsurface Features
1. Geological: geologic history of the area, bedrock type, depth to bedrock, geologic texture
2. Hydrology: aquifers, underground river, springs, water table
3. Soil: genesis, classifications or types, fertility, erosion susceptibility, temperature, moisture (pF), reaction (pH), typical horizons, aeration, texture, organic content, bearing capacity

Natural Surface Features
1. Vegetation: type or variety, size, location, shade patterns, aesthetic value, ecological community
2. Slopes: gradients, landforms, elevations, drainage patterns
3. Hydrology: flood plains; rivers, lakes, marsh, streams, bogs, watershed; drainage patterns
4. Wildlife: ecology, species
5. Climate: precipitation—annual snow and rain; potential for mist or low-lying fog; humidity; wind direction, intensity; solar orientation; temperature—average, highest, and lowest

Cultural and Man-Made Features
1. Utilities: location; types—sanitary, water, gas, electric, storm drains; depth or height of each structure; condition
2. Land use: present use of site adjacent to the site, zoning restrictions, legal restrictions, legal ownership of the site, boundary lines, easement
3. Historical notes: archeological sites; landmarks; building type, size, condition
4. Circulation: linkages and transit (road), on or near the site; auto and pedestrian; bicycle, boat, mass transit
5. Social factors: population, intensity, distribution, age composition, educational level, income level, ethnic or type; economic and political factors; social configurations of the residents; usage of the area; other social factors affecting usage of the area

Aesthetic Factors
1. Perceptual: from an auto, by pedestrian, from a bicycle
2. Spatial pattern: views to the site; views from the site; spaces—existing, potential for new areas; sequential relationships
3. Natural features: significant natural features of the site; water elements, rock formations, plant material

EXAMPLES: Figures 9-6 and 9-7.

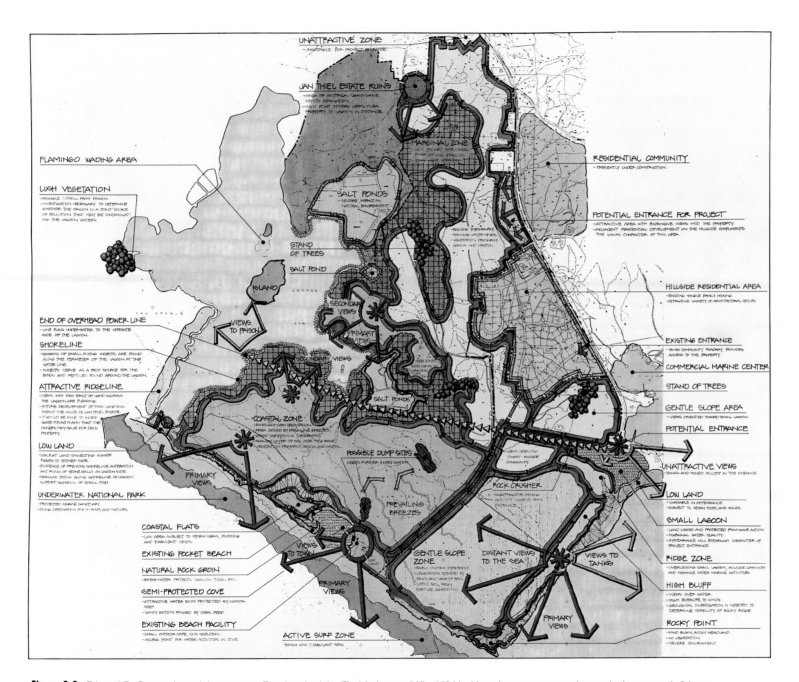

Figure 9-6. Edward D. Stone, Jr. and Associates, Fort Lauderdale, FL. Marker on 20″ × 30″ blackline diazo print paper (original ink on sepia). 8 hours.

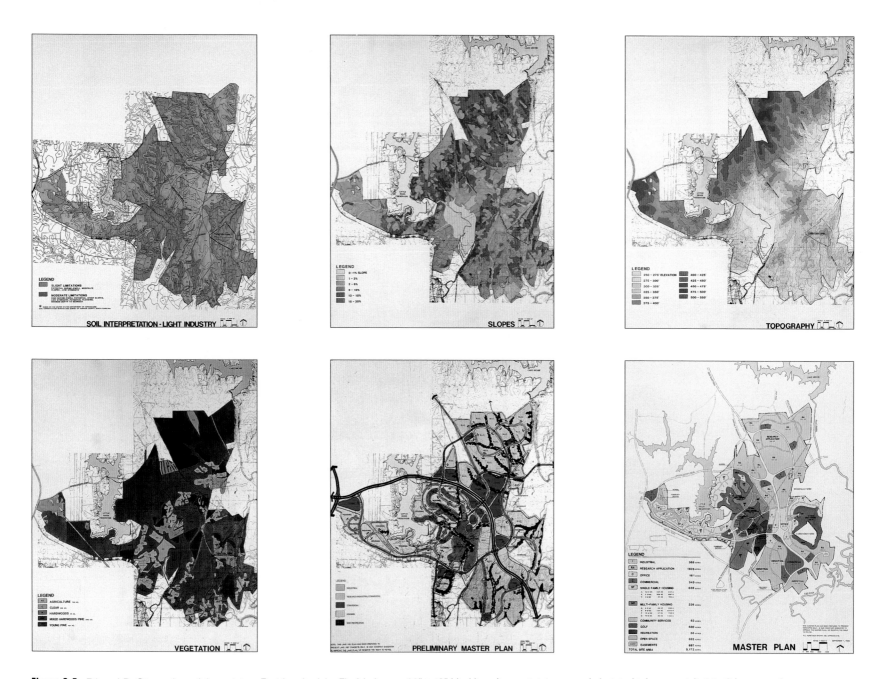

Figure 9-7. Edward D. Stone, Jr. and Associates, Fort Lauderdale, FL. Marker on 30″ × 42″ blackline diazo print paper each (original ink on sepia). 4 to 8 hours each.

DEVELOP DESIGN CONCEPTS

When designing a project, the designer must be able to present the design concept graphically, incorporating the results of earlier stages. The space relationships from bubble diagrams and the facts from site inventories and analysis form the basis for study. The established information can be analyzed, diagnosed, and synthesized to formulate an optimum solution. This is then illustrated in concept diagrams, character sketches, and concept statements.

The concept diagrams incorporate the information from bubble diagrams and site analysis into an actual site plan. Once the concept diagrams have been established, loose character sketches are added to express the designer's ideas. Finally, written statements sum up the established programs, the design problems, and their solutions.

EXAMPLES: Figures 9-8 and 9-9.

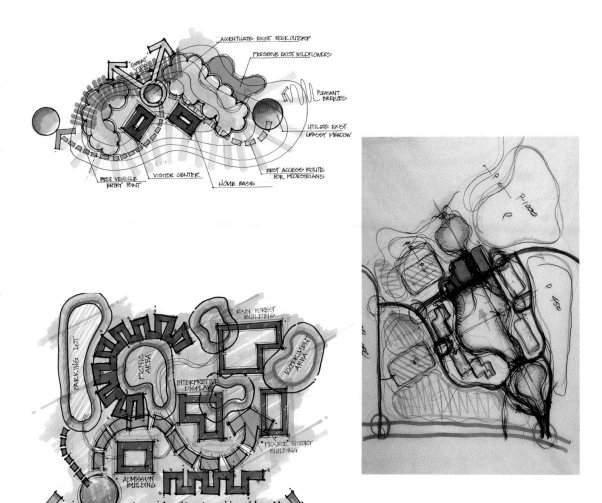

Figure 9-8. Left: participants, ML Graphic Workshop. Marker, colored pencil, and felt-tip pen on 19″ × 24″ marker paper. 1½ hours. Right: Ken Cobb, Johnson, Johnson & Roy Inc, Ann Arbor, MI. Marker on 20″ × 30″ white tracing paper.

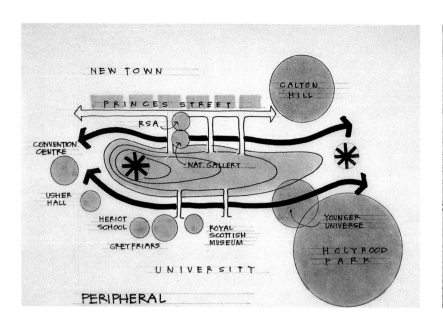

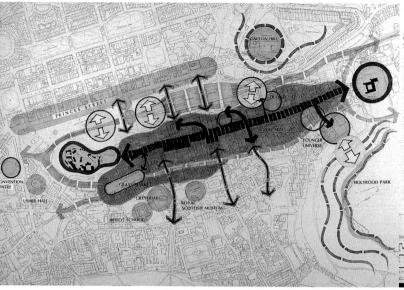

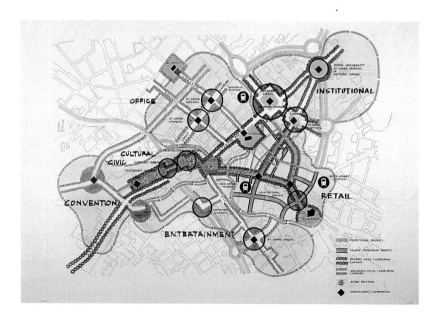

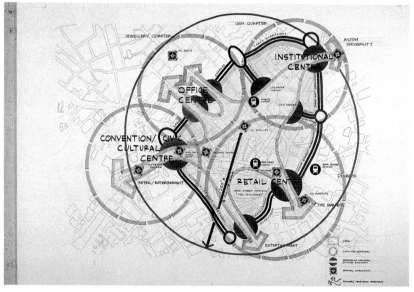

Figure 9-9. Land Design/Research, Inc, Columbia, MD. Marker and felt-tip pen on 12″ × 18″ tracing and blackline diazo print paper each (original ink on vellum). 30 minutes to 3 hours each.

CHOOSE A DESIGN APPROACH

A successful design presentation usually follows one of six basic approaches: rectilinear, rectilinear-45, radial, arc and tangent, irregular, and curvilinear. These fundamental design forms all use a grid system to give a sense of scale and guide designers to the final design solution. Each design approach also has its own characteristics.

These approaches provide simple steps that save time and result in better design to fit the client's needs. They are a way to polish and refine the design.

They are not, however, the absolute only way to approach a design-form solution. After becoming familiar with each approach, you can mix the design "rules" and combine two or more of the approaches.

The six design approaches are arranged in figures 9-10 to 9-15 from the simplest and easiest to the most complex and difficult to produce. In each case, the basic definition is given, followed by the essential characteristics, the grid used, and key symbols. This will help you to match an approach to a project. For example, if your client's needs are traditional and formal, you might decide on the rectilinear approach. Finally, in each case, three different drawings based on this approach sum up design concept proposals.

A checklist of the principles of design approaches that are discussed in depth in this section follows. For an application on a sample site plan, see figure 9-16.

TWENTY-THREE PRINCIPLES
1. Parallel lines
2. Perpendicular intersection
3. Vanish to a point
4. Line up
5. Project/recess
6. Width variations
7. Height variations
8. Size variations
9. Repeat shape
10. Proportional Method
11. Compound curve
12. Material connect

13. Avoid falsely implied lines
14. Avoid spotty elements
15. Avoid sharp corners
16. Avoid recognizable shapes
17. Avoid small/wrong scale
18. Axis
19. Focal point
20. Contrast
21. Asymmetrical
22. Mass/void
23. Zig-zag

The principles discussed below will add to the dynamism of a design concept organization. Some are recommended specifically for certain approaches, but most are applicable to all. Some are things to avoid in your work; others make positive contributions. All should be studied and applied in conjunction with the forty-five principles of good graphics (see chapter 2).

RECTILINEAR

A rectilinear design
approach uses vertical
and horizontal lines
on a square grid.

Grid/Key Symbol

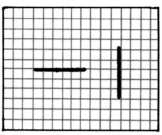

CHARACTERISTICS

Dominant	Easy	Directional	Forceful
Quick	Logical	Strong	Defined
Orderly	Expected	Rigid	Static
Basic	Sterile		

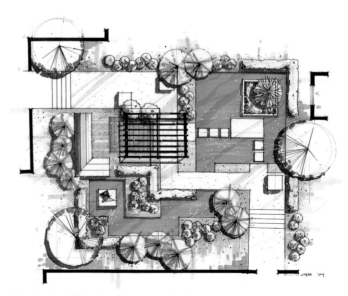

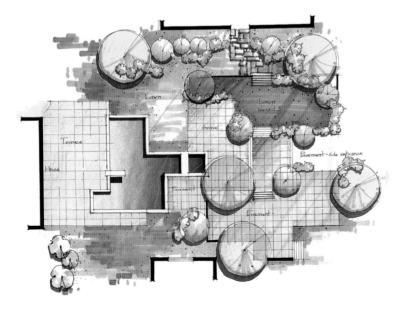

Figure 9-10. Top right: designed by Debbie Graviss, rendered by Audrey Hyde. Bottom left: participant, ML Graphic Workshop. Bottom right: designed and rendered by Siew-Lian Chua. Participant, ML Graphic Workshop. Marker, colored pencil, felt-tip pen, and airbrush on 19″ × 24″ marker paper. Design, 40 minutes each, rendering 1 to 2 hours each.

RECTILINEAR-45

A rectilinear-45 design approach introduces vertical, horizontal, and 45-degree lines on a square grid.

Grid/Key Symbol

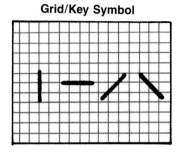

CHARACTERISTICS

Dynamic	Active	Exciting	Bold
Intense	Jagged	Strong	Vigorous
Various	Tense	Fast	Connecting

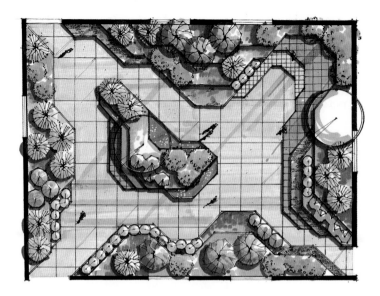

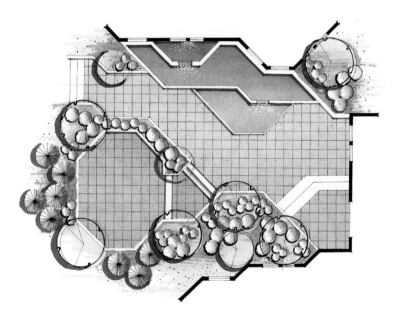

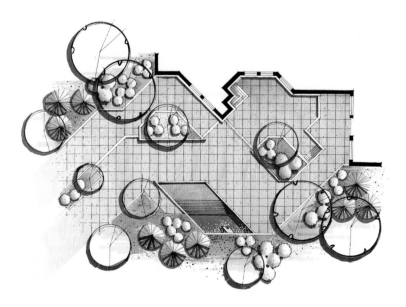

Figure 9-11. Top right: designed and rendered by Kate Drucke. Bottom left: designed by Nicote Panaccione, rendered by Stephen Clay. Bottom right: designed by Doug Abbott, rendered by Russ Richey. Participants, ML Graphic Workshop. Marker, colored pencil, felt-tip pen and airbrush on 19″ × 24″ marker paper. Design, 40 minutes each; rendering, 1 to 2 hours each.

RADIAL

A radial design approach uses various sizes of circles that branch out from a central point and multidirectional straight lines on a radial grid.

Grid/Key Symbol

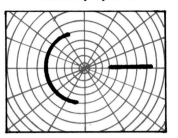

CHARACTERISTICS

Intense	Spiral	Bold	Mysterious
Interesting	Expanding	Flamboyant	Concentrating
Directional	Progressive	Attractive	Mazelike
Developing	Strong		

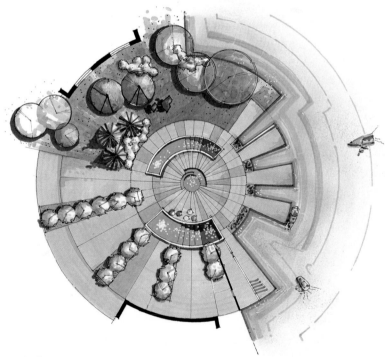

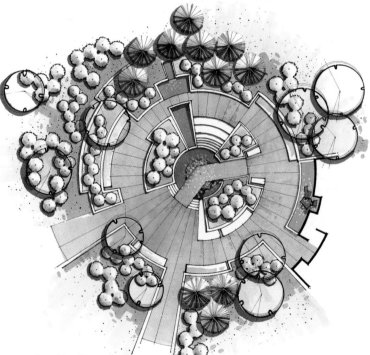

Figure 9-12. Top right: rendered by Kevin Marshall. Bottom left: designed by Eleanor Mckinney, rendered by Roger Greidanus. Bottom right: designed by Gylynn Moten, rendered by Michelle Flynn. Participants, ML Graphic Workshop. Marker, colored pencil, felt-tip pen, airbrush, and pastel on 19″ × 24″ marker paper. Design, 40 minutes each; rendering 1 to 2 hours each.

ARC-AND-TANGENT

An arc-and-tangent
design approach is
comprised of horizontal,
vertical, and 45-degree
lines, and quarter,
half, three-quarter,
and full circles
on a square grid.

Grid/Key Symbol

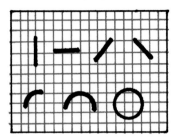

CHARACTERISTICS

Soft	Inviting	Refined	Pleasing
Flowing	Formal	Compromise	Passive
Soothing	Transitional	Smooth	

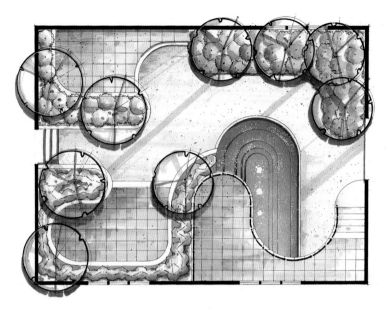

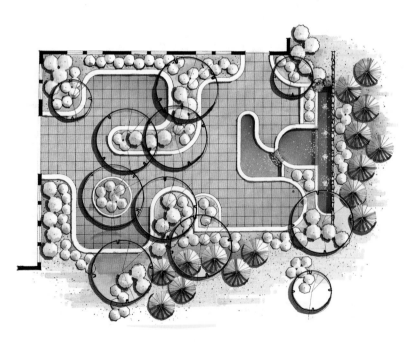

Figure 9-13. Top right: designed by Doug Abbott, rendered by Christine Hess. Bottom left: designed by Susan Bardwell, rendered by Roger Greidanus. Bottom right: rendered by Stephen Clay. Participants, ML Graphic Workshop. Marker, colored pencil, felt-tip pen, and airbrush on 19″ × 24″ marker paper. Design, 40 minutes each; rendering, 1 to 2 hours each.

IRREGULAR

An irregular design
approach contains vertical,
horizontal, 45-degree,
and multidirectional lines
on a square grid.

Grid/Key Symbol

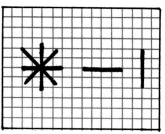

CHARACTERISTICS

Asymmetrical	Exciting	Shifting	Complex
Interesting	Various	Fluctuating	Dynamic
Diverse	Active	Irregular	Unique
Nontraditional	Surprising	Uncertain	Intriguing

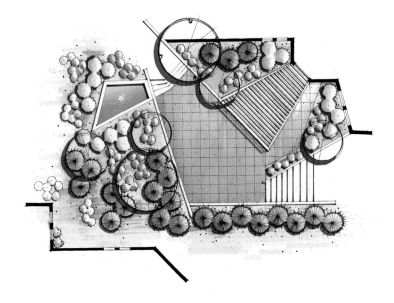

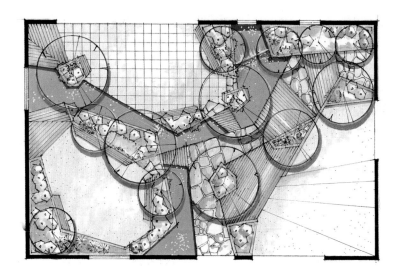

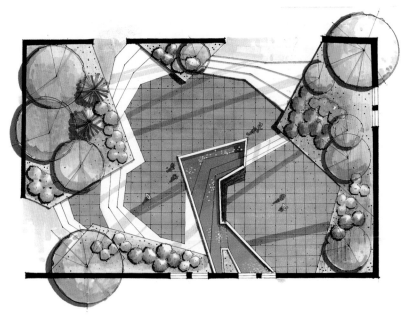

Figure 9-14. Top right: rendered by Kevin Marshall. Bottom left: designed and rendered by Buck Brader. Bottom right: designed and rendered by Audrey Hyde. Participants, ML Graphic Workshop. Marker, colored pencil, felt-tip pen and airbrush on 19″ × 24″ marker paper. Design, 40 minutes each; rendering, 1 to 2 hours each.

CURVILINEAR

A curvilinear design approach
consists of compound
curves and the absence
of straight lines
on a square grid.

Grid/Key Symbol

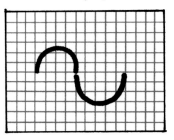

CHARACTERISTICS

Fluid	Flowing	Sensual	Nontraditional
Soft	Beautiful	Serene	Casual
Rolling	Organic	Intimate	Continual
Interesting	Spiritual	Relaxed	Pleasant
Graceful	Delicate		

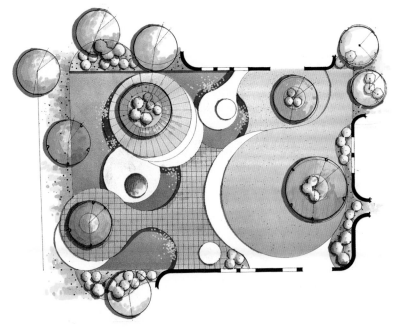

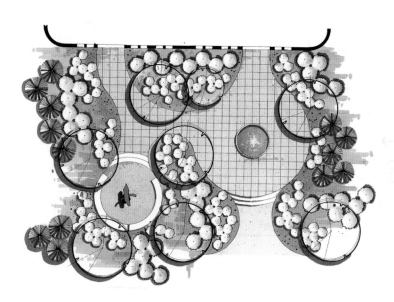

Figure 9-15. Top right: designed by Buck Brader, rendered by Russ Richey. Bottom left: designed by Scott Milne, rendered by Debbie Graviss. Bottom right: designed by Miguel Iraola, rendered by Cara Silliman. Participants, ML Graphic Workshop. Marker, colored pencil, felt-tip pen, and airbrush on 19″ × 24″ marker paper. Design, 40 minutes each; rendering, 1 to 2 hours each.

DESIGN APPROACH PRINCIPLES

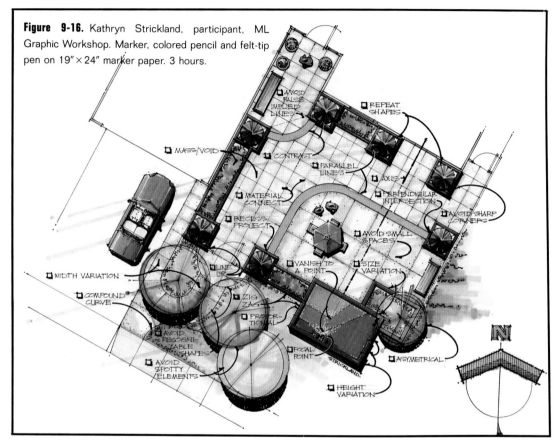

Figure 9-16. Kathryn Strickland, participant, ML Graphic Workshop. Marker, colored pencil and felt-tip pen on 19″ × 24″ marker paper. 3 hours.

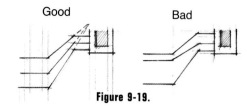

Figure 9-19.

3. Vanish to a Point

Lines vanish to a common point. This creates a rhythm and focal point that is dynamic and subconsciously perceived.

APPLICATION: radial, irregular

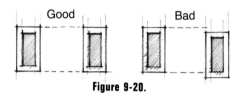

Figure 9-20.

4. Line Up

Elements in the space line up beside or behind each other. This creates an organized, straight, clean, systematic, and eye-pleasing effect. If you do offset elements, exaggerate the offset for better composition.

APPLICATION: all design approaches

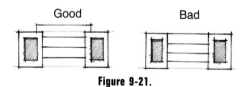

Figure 9-21.

5. Project/Recess

An object that projects or is recessed from other elements, such as a step to a planter, gives a more three-dimensional appearance. It casts shadows and creates zig-zag and interest. The finished piece is also more durable when constructed.

APPLICATION: all design approaches

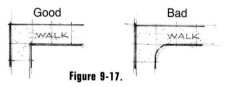

Figure 9-17.

1. Parallel Lines

Two adjacent lines are parallel to each other. This helps to create harmony and unity in design.

APPLICATION: rectilinear, rectilinear-45, radial, arc-and-tangent, irregular

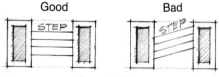

Figure 9-18.

2. Perpendicular Intersection

Two lines intersect at a 90-degree angle. This provides maximum use of space, gives a strong bold feeling, and makes the project easier to build.

APPLICATION: all design approaches

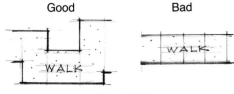

Figure 9-22.

6. Width Variations

Spaces are not all the same width. Walkways and adjacent planters, for example, in a plaza area, are more interesting and will zig-zag if they are of different width dimensions. *APPLICATION:* all design approaches

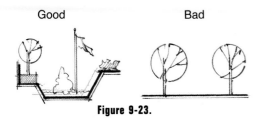

Figure 9-23.

7. Height Variations

Elements are different heights. This creates a vertical zig-zag and adds interest to a space. Height variations can be obtained through the use of steps, planters, canopies, poles, trees, and fountains.
APPLICATION: all design approaches

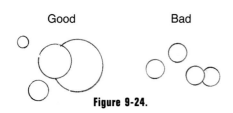

Figure 9-24.

8. Size Variations

Repeat a shape but vary the size. This creates interest, contrast, and rhythm.
APPLICATION: all design approaches

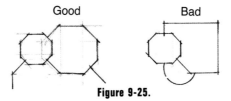

Figure 9-25.

9. Repeat Shape

Repeat a shape in different sizes to create rhythm and harmony.
APPLICATION: all design approaches

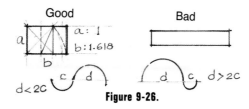

Figure 9-26.

10. Proportional Method

Proportional method is based on the relationship of one dimension to another. For example, the Golden Mean describes a rectangle with a 1-to-1.618 ratio of width to length, and the Fabinitz theory depicts a compound curve with a 1 to 2 or less ratio. Such ratios can be used to achieve correct proportions in spaces.
APPLICATION: rectilinear, rectilinear-45, arc-and-tangent, curvilinear

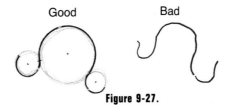

Figure 9-27.

11. Compound Curve

A compound curve uses various-size circles without a straight line in between them. This creates a smooth and flowing design.
APPLICATION: curvilinear

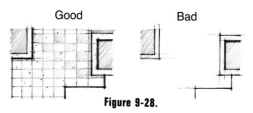

Figure 9-28.

12. Material Connect

Use a building material such as a paving pattern to tie spaces together. This creates unity, totality, mass/void, and eye-pleasing effect. *APPLICATION:* all design approaches

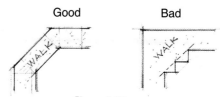

Figure 9-29.

13. Avoid Falsely Implied Lines

The continuous repetition of a shape will falsely imply a line that conflicts with an adjacent line. This breaks the principle of parallel line discussed earlier.
APPLICATION: all design approaches

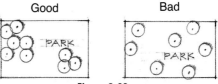

Figure 9-30.

14. Avoid Spotty Elements

Spotty elements such as randomly positioned trees, planters, benches, and paving patterns often create visual chaos, thus losing the principle of focal point and mass/void. *APPLICATION:* all design approaches

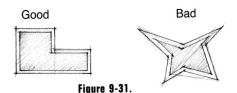

Good   Bad

Figure 9-31.

15. Avoid Sharp Corners

Sharp corners, those with less than a 45-degree angle, are more expensive to build and more hazardous, and on the inside of the building collect trash easily.

APPLICATION: radial, irregular

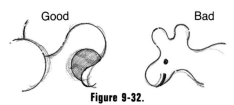

Good   Bad

Figure 9-32.

16. Avoid Recognizable Shapes

Recognizable shapes are distracting in a design. Avoid using the shape of a life form that is familiar to people (such as a simulation of a dog, a kidney, or the face of a person). The shape of a creative design should be original rather than derived from familiar shapes.

APPLICATION: all design approaches

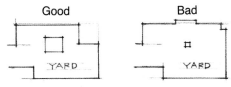

Good   Bad

Figure 9-33.

17. Avoid Small/Wrong Scale

A very small space in a design is out of scale and can be impractical in reality. A 2-foot-wide planter or fountain, for example, in a large space would be lost while a 2-foot-wide sidewalk would be too narrow for even two people to walk side-by-side.

APPLICATION: all design approaches

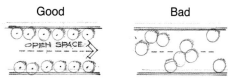

Good   Bad

Figure 9-34.

18. Axis

An axis is a large, open path that gives a sense of direction, draws one in, and helps to accent a focal point.

APPLICATION: all design approaches

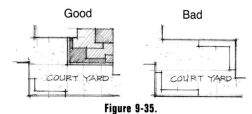

Good   Bad

Figure 9-35.

19. Focal Point

A focal point is a feature attraction, such as a fountain or piece of sculpture, created to draw people into a space. It does not necessarily have to be located in the center of a space. *APPLICATION*: all design approaches

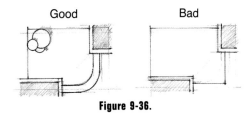

Good   Bad

Figure 9-36.

20. Contrast

A contrast is a gentle, workable conflict between elements, used to accent a focal point and create interest. Such elements include opposite shapes, varying texture, size, color, line, and value.

APPLICATION: all design approaches

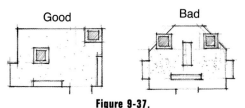

Good   Bad

Figure 9-37.

21. Asymmetrical

An asymmetrical design is a proportionally balanced design that does not use symmetry (a mirror image of one side). Asymmetry creates interest and dynamism in a design.

APPLICATION: all design approaches

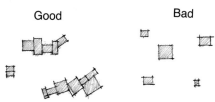

Good   Bad

Figure 9-38.

22. Mass/Void

Mass and void are two groups of elements that allow a design to work and can help to avoid spottiness. For example, a group of trees is a mass and grass is a void.

APPLICATION: all design approaches

Good   Bad

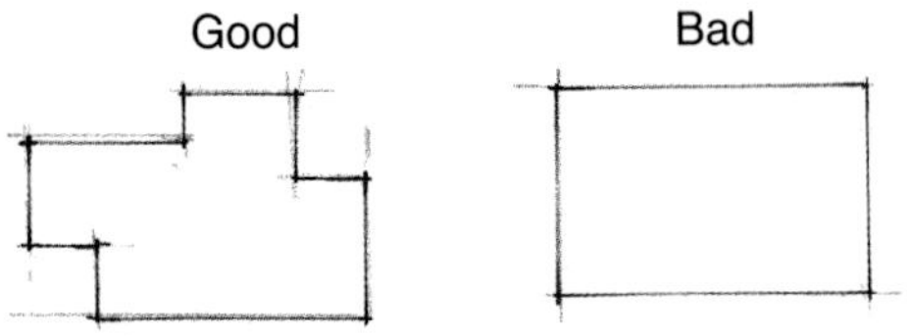

Figure 9-39.

23. Zig-Zag

Zig-zag is used to avoid monotony in the overall shape of the design. It improves the composition of a project.

APPLICATION: all design approaches

PRESENT DESIGN SOLUTIONS

Design ideas begin in the mind of a creative designer. Once the original idea is formulated, it must be communicated to become reality: verbally, in written statements, and through graphic presentation. Visual graphics are most important: they are easiest for the client to comprehend. Plans, elevations, sections, renderings, and models are all presentation elements. Each is described below, with various technical tips included.

PLAN GRAPHICS

Plan graphics are the most widely used form of presentation graphics. They show the site or plan from an overhead, aerial perspective and present spacial relationships clearly to the client. These are also the drawings which will later provide a basis for any construction drawing documentation.

Plan graphics are customarily first completed on mylar or vellum using pencil or pen and then printed on diazo print paper and colored. Spatial relationships between buildings, pedestrian and vehicular circulation, vegetation and other natural features are stressed. Plan graphics, though somewhat symbolic at times, should not be predominantly abstract. Entourage elements should be combined to depict an overhead view of their design.

Technical Tips

• Always apply color to the prints and copies of the original and not the original vellum. That way you may reprint the original if necessary.
• When using media which may fade, such as marker or Sharpie on vellum, always run a reverse sepia print immediately following

completion. This will give you a preserved original to use for multiple prints.
• For ease of reference, the plan should usually be oriented with north straight up.
• When drawing the final plan view, use different line weights in pen or pencil. This differentiates objects on the plan and assists in the depiction of depth (fig. 9-40).
• Some features in the plan should be labeled. Make labels parallel to the lines of the feature they are identifying (fig. 9-41).
• Adding shadow to the plan view gives the plan depth and shows elevation changes. Shadows are usually the darkest feature of the plan and should be added carefully so as not to obscure important details. Although black is recommended, many times gray may be used to keep details readable and to avoid a spotty appearance.
• The quickest way to project shadows is to slip a second print under the one you are working on and shift it down and to the left or right. This will help to establish an accurate and consistent shadow pattern. A light table makes this very easy to do.
• Entourage such as cars, trees, figures, and other details will give the plan a more realistic and lively look.
• Use both red and black pencils on vellum or mylar applications. The red pencil will print about 60 percent as dark as the black graphite pencil, causing subtle value changes in the plan. It is most appropriate for ground plane elements such as grass and will give a two-color quality to the original (fig. 9-42).
• Use a circle template to locate plantings and add symbols to identify trees as either deciduous or coniferous. As a rule no more than three different symbols should be used in any one plan view. Trees should always include shadows unless they cover up important features or details.

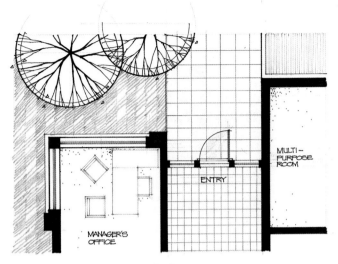

Figure 9-40.

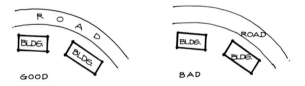

Figure 9-41.

Figure 9-42.

• Value changes may also be achieved by affixing vellum overlays cut to size to the original before printing. The added layers print slightly darker than a single sheet (fig. 9-43).

• When using a marker to color prints, draw stripes on the ground plane, grass, and paving areas. They should run in the same direction as shadows to reinforce their appearance.

• Stippling, or the use of dots, is also appropriate for grass and concrete areas. Stippling should usually be the heaviest near the perimeter of any surface. An airbrush on low pressure will spatter and create a very pleasing stippling effect.

• Information in a "title-block" label should include the name and address of the project, names of client and designer, date, "north" arrow, scale, logo, and when appropriate a legend and sheet number.

• Always put the title block on the right side or bottom of the sheet. This will depend upon how the sheets will eventually be read. If more sheets are to be packaged and represented horizontally, the bottom will be more appropriate.

• Use press-on letters for a more formal appearance. Trace letters from press-on letter forms to give a loose quality to the drawing (fig. 9-44).

• Use the same style of press-on lettering throughout the entire project. Size should reflect the importance of the subject. The title of the project is usually the largest size lettering.

EXAMPLES: Figures 9-45 to 9-48.

Original   Print

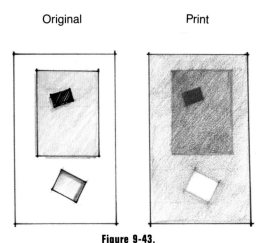

Figure 9-43.

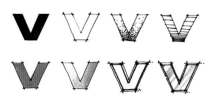

Figure 9-44.

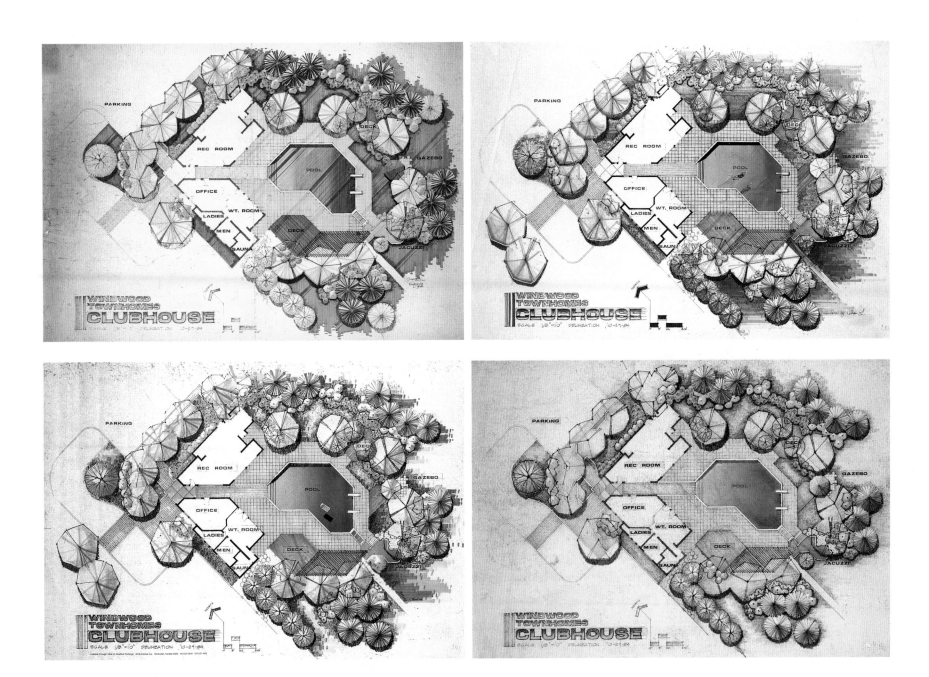

Figure 9-45. Rendered by, top left: D. Steinke; top right: Guy Faber; bottom left: William Lin; bottom right: Todd F., participants, ML Graphic Workshop. Marker, colored pencil, and airbrush on 24″ × 36″ blackline diazo print paper. 3 hours each.

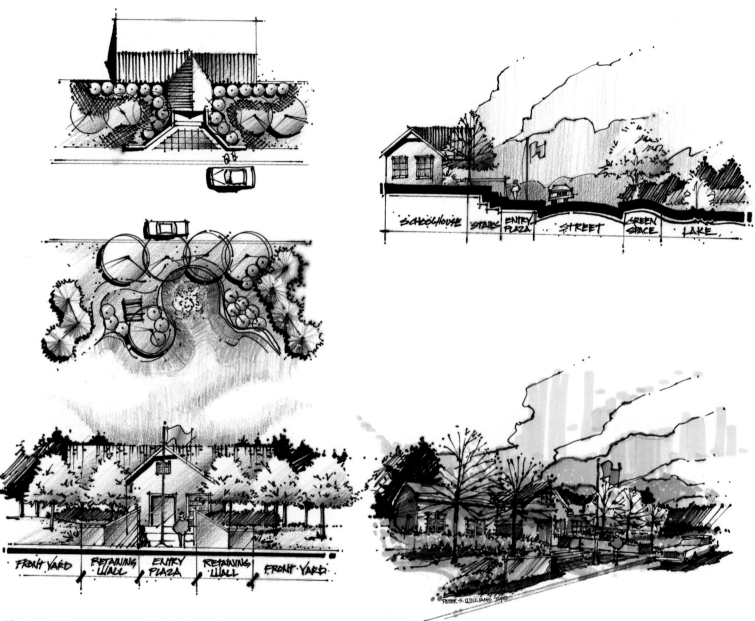

Labels within images:

SCHOOLHOUSE | STAIRS | ENTRY PLAZA | STREET | GREEN SPACE | LAKE

FRONT YARD | RETAINING WALL | ENTRY PLAZA | RETAINING WALL | FRONT YARD

PETER S. WILLIAMS 7/90

Figure 9-46. Peter Williams, participant, ML Graphic workshop. Marker, colored pencil, and felt-tip pen on 19" × 24" marker paper. 4 hours.

Figure 9-47. Shannon Gordon, Bloodgood Architects, Inc., Des Moines, IA. Marker and colored pencil on 24″ × 36″ blackline diazo print paper (original, pen and ink on mylar). 14 hours.

ELEVATIONS

The elevation is the face of a building. Elevations use a front-plane depiction, including all of the elements that fall on and behind this plane. In many ways the elevation is like a modified one-point perspective. It is often used in place of a final perspective illustration.

Architects use elevations to depict proposed building facades and their elements. Elevations are usually produced directly from the floor or site plan and may be used to show the overall front, back, or sides of any building and site treatment.

Technical Tips

• Usually the chosen scale of the elevation should be the same as the plan view.
• Scale should always be noted under the elevation. Also note if there is exaggeration in the vertical scale.
• Shade and shadow give a three-dimensional appearance, and including some sky in the elevation can enliven the entire view.
• Use a heavy thick line to represent the ground line. Special effects may be achieved by extending the ground plane forward in the elevation, giving the illusion of a one-point perspective.
• When rendering elevations in color, strive for appropriate value changes to create the illusion of depth. Also add stripes and dots to enhance the textures being represented and to add interest.
• Press-on letters may be used to represent signage.

EXAMPLES: Figures 9-48 to 9-50.

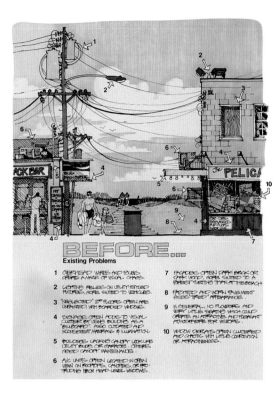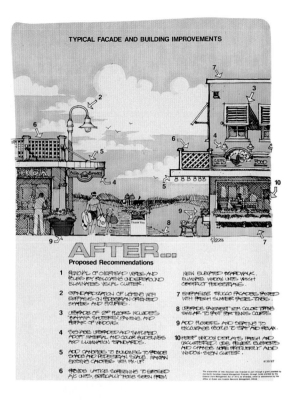

Figure 9-48. Edward D. Stone, Jr. and Associates, Fort Lauderdale, FL. Marker on 30″ × 42″ blackline diazo print paper (original, felt-tip pen on white tracing paper). 8 hours.

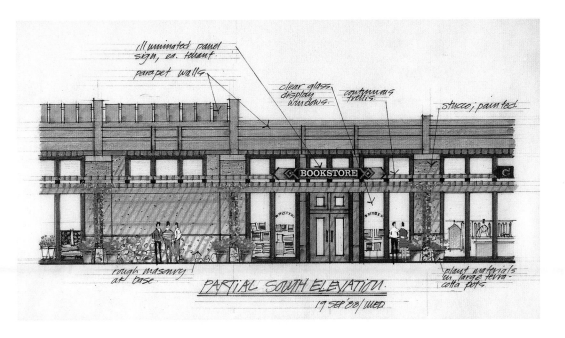

illuminated panel
sign, ea. tenant.

parapet walls.

clear glass
display
windows.

continuous
trellis.

stucco; painted

BOOKSTORE

rough masonry
at base

plant materials
in large terra-
cotta pots

PARTIAL SOUTH ELEVATION.
19 SEP '88/ WED.

Vary window mullion
treatments within
4' module.

Vary transom
treatments.

Add cornice/reglet
treatments.

Add "header"
(color change)
where no
trellis exists.

REVISION STUDY, ELEV. thru COURTS, looking SOUTH
⅛"=1'-0"
9 DEC 8'/ WED

Figure 9-49. Michael E. Doyle, Boulder, CO. Marker, colored pencil, and felt-tip pen on 5½" × 10" to 8" × 17" white tracing paper. 45 minutes to 8 hours.

Figure 9-50. Chad Moor, Bloodgood Architects, Inc., Des Moines, IA. Marker and colored pencil on 24″ × 36″ blackline diazo print paper (original, pen and ink on mylar). 6 hours.

SECTIONS

Sections are cutaway views to show the relationship of horizontal and vertical elements of plan and elevation. They are often easier to understand than plan views and allow designers to project their ideas quickly.

Sectional views are two-dimensional. They are especially useful when showing vertical changes including steps and walls, along with the interrelationship of areas not easily shown in plan or elevation. Landscape architects use sections to portray topography changes as they relate to the built environment. Architects and interior designers find it most useful in showing the inside relationships of different rooms and their details within any one building.

Sections are normally drawn at the same horizontal scale as the plan view. There are three basic types (fig. 9-51):

1. **Regular Section.** This shows only the elements which lie directly on the chosen viewing plane. It is best for quick, loose, schematic sketches.

2. **Section-Elevation.** In addition to the elements shown in a regular section, this view includes elements behind the plane. It is frequently used for architectural purposes.

3. **Sectional-Perspective.** This incorporates depth through the addition of a perspective to a regular section and is appropriate for architectural and landscape forms.

Technical Tips

• Cut the section where it will reveal the essence of the design. The horizontal scale should be the same as that of the plan. The vertical scale, however, can be exaggerated to emphasize changes in elevation. This exaggeration is particularly important when dealing with large-scale areas.

• Always refer to the plan view when drawing sections and identify the direction in

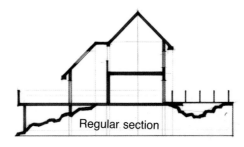

Regular section

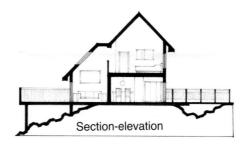

Section-elevation

Section-perspective

Figure 9-51.

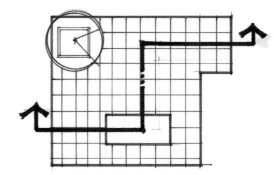

Figure 9-52.

Figure 9-53.

which you are looking. When necessary, the cutting plane of the section may be moved back and forth to show desired elements accordingly (fig. 9-52).

• Always draw a 3-D line on the bottom of the section (fig. 9-53).

EXAMPLES: Figures 9-54 to 9-56.

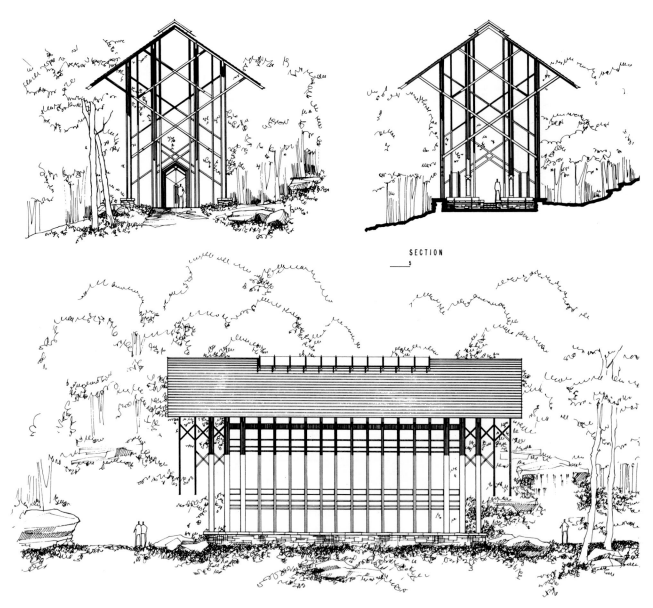

SECTION
5

Figure 9-54. Fay Jones & Maurice Jennings Architects, Fayetteville, AR. Pen and Ink on 24" × 36" vellum. 24 hours.

visable site

shelter will be located periodically

the palm lined portion of Palmetto Avenue will be preserved as part of the

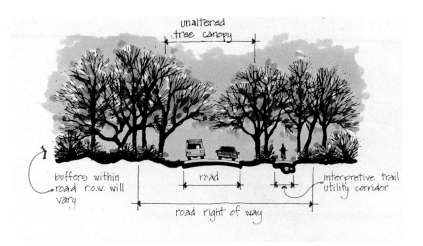

unaltered tree canopy

buffers within road r.o.w. will vary.

road

interpretive trail utility corridor

road right of way

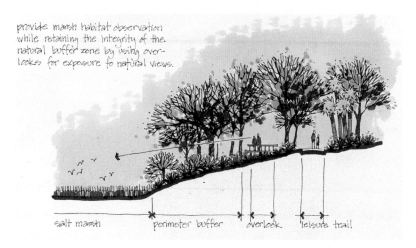

provide marsh habitat observation while retaining the integrity of the natural buffer zone by using overlooks for exposure to natural views.

salt marsh   perimeter buffer   overlook   leisure trail

Figure 9-55. Edward D. Stone, Jr. and Associates, Fort Lauderdale, FL. Marker on 8½″ × 11″ blackline diazo print paper each. (original felt-tip pen on white tracing paper). 1 hour each.

Figure 9-56. Peter Williams, participant, ML Graphic Workshop. Marker, color pencil, felt-tip pen and airbrush on 19″ × 24″ marker paper. 6 hours.

RENDERING

A rendering is a representational or perspective drawing that presents the final design as it will appear once built. It is an important presentation tool because it shows the client clearly what the final design product will look like. It can significantly influence the acceptance of a project by the client.

It requires great skill and is time-consuming to complete. For this reason many people shy away from it.

The key to rendering is having confidence and practicing your skills. The more renderings you do, the better you will become. When approaching the final rendering, it is advisable to work with good-quality art material. Quality materials and sufficient time help to ensure a refined final product.

Do not always try the same media technique when approaching the final rendering. The basic principles involved in producing a successful rendering are often the same. A clear understanding of the forty-five principles of good graphics outlined in chapter 2 will allow you to use a variety of media. The matrix chart outlining techniques and media will provide you with a way to choose according to your capabilities and the desires of the client. By matching media to technique, you will be able to express your design in the most favorable manner. Be confident and patient in approaching final renderings. Many times you may be unsure of its success until the final touches are added. Don't give up; this is critical.

Technical Tips

• Size of the final rendering should also conform to the client's desires; however, smaller renderings are usually more quickly and easily completed.
• The best view for the final rendering is usually at eye level and from a direction that conveys the concepts most important to the design.
• Generally, colored renderings are preferred by the client. Sometimes future reproduction of the drawing may warrant the use of black and white media techniques.
• Always seek client approval of a preliminary rough draft for the angle of view, composition, color selection, and so on before completing a final rendering.
• Use entourage elements—trees, figures, and cars—to give the drawing a realistic look. Entourage can also be used to cover areas that may be beyond your skills. Always include mature trees and shrubs. Portray the drawing in the most favorable manner possible.
• Be willing to spend time and money to achieve a successful final rendering.
• Choose the best paper and materials for any chosen medium and technique.
• Do not overwork the final rendering. Budget your time and complete it accordingly. Often a rendering is ruined by being overworked.
• Framing the final rendering in a good quality mat board or other appropriate material will enhance its quality.

EXAMPLES: Figures 9-57 to 9-60.

MODELS

Models present concepts and ideas in three dimensions. They allow the client to walk around the design and view it from different perspectives quickly. Most people relate well to models.

There are two kinds of models available: a rough, or study, model and a presentation model. The study model is built with rough textured materials during a preliminary stage of the design. It allows the designer to work with three dimensions and to visualize the project before he is committed too far. The presentation model is much more refined. It takes skill, time, and quality material to generate a lifelike appearance.

Technical Tips

• Change your knife blades often. Always use a sturdy straightedge for cutting.
• Use a sheet of vinyl as a cutting base to achieve smooth edges. (This will also conserve blades.)
• Use corrugated cardboard or foam board for contours and affix pins with adhesive to hold the contours in place.
• Use computer imagery to generate facades, etc., then paste them to the structure of the building model to better visualize the finished product.
• When photographing models, use a blue background material as the sky when shooting indoors, or photograph against the sky to create realism when shooting outdoors.
• Consider a detachable roof so that the entire project—interior included—is accessible.
• Buy commercially made trees, figures, cars, and furniture, to add realism when building presentation models.
• Add additional buildings to the model site, those that are on site but not part of your design, using rough, blocked-out forms, adding detail only to those buildings that are relevant to your design.
• Construct buildings directly on the site plan to eliminate the need for actual contours, while still giving an idea of what the site will look like.

EXAMPLE: Figure 9-61.

Figure 9-57. Jay Kabriel, Annapolis, MD. Left: Watercolor on 24″×36″ watercolor board. 30 hours. Right: watercolor on 18″×24″ watercolor paper. 6 hours.

Figure 9-58. Howard Needles Tammen & Bergendoff, Kansas City, MO. Right: watercolor on 24″ × 24″ watercolor paper (original, pen and ink on vellum). 26 hours. Left: watercolor on 36″ × 18″ watercolor paper (original, pen and ink on vellum). 12 hours.

Figure 9-59. Left: Michael Worobec, Land Design/Research, Inc, Columbia, MD. Marker and colored pencil on 24″ × 36″ blackline diazo print paper (original, pen and ink on vellum). 40 hours. Right: Bill Renick Cincinnati, OH, for RTKL. Gouache on 20″ × 30″ illustration board. 10 hours.

Figure 9-60. Top left: Dick Sneary, Kansas City, MO. Colored pencil and watercolor on 12″ × 16″ watercolor paper (original, pen and ink on vellum). 40 to 50 hours. Top right: Andrew King, Decatur, GA. Watercolor on 14″ × 30″ watercolor board paper. 12 hours. Bottom left: Prelim & Associates, Dallas, TX. Gouache on 11″ × 14″ illustration board. 28 hours. Bottom right: Art Associates, Toledo, OH. Casein on 12″ × 18″ watercolor board. 30 hours.

Figure 9-61. Top: participants, ML Graphic Workshop. 20″ × 20″ and 20″ × 30″. 45 hours each. Bottom left: Rick Strawn, Howard Needles Tammen & Bergendoff, Kansas City, MO. 24″ × 36″. 140 hours. Bottom right: RTKL Associates Inc., Baltimore, MD. 36″ × 36″. 220 hours.

A Case Study

This case study focuses on the redesign of a public courtyard located in Kansas City, Missouri. It is 160 feet by 120 feet. Its south side faces the main street and its three other sides are surrounded by a four-story historical office building. The ground floor of the building has an Italian restaurant on the north side and shops on the west side. Through an interview with the developer, and site analysis, and subsequent investigations into local codes and zoning regulations have been researched, the designer isolated several important features out of which the design program began to emerge.

- shopping center—store
- a public space—crowd
- semiprivate spaces—peaceful
- private spaces—quiet
- parking lot, sidewalk
- primary circulation
- secondary circulation
- seating—benches, planters, grass, edge of water fountain
- food—cafe, vendors
- entertainment—jugglers, band, etc.
- focal point—water feature, sculpture
- color—flowering vegetation, banners, flags, canopies
- grade change—steps, ramps, stage
- texture—paving, brick, planting, cobble, scoring
- view to and from the building
- security—lighting, gates
- historical features—details

After establishing the program, the designer looks for program relationships between the spaces that can then be transferred to bubble diagrams.

PUBLIC SPACE: main circulation space, magnetic focal point, connection to buildings, parking, vending.

SEMIPRIVATE: water, connection to public space, vegetation, tables and chairs.

PRIVATE: screen, benches.

FOOD: cafe, restaurant.

SHOPPING: store.

PARKING: lot, sidewalk.

BUBBLE DIAGRAMS TO RENDERING

After finding program relationships, two relationship bubble diagrams are studied and the positive and negative features are identified. A revised bubble diagram is then drawn showing the ideal relationships in graphic form (fig. 9-62). The site inventories, such as views, circulation, climate, topography, vegetation, and utilities are merged to establish a site analysis (fig. 9-63). By laying the bubble diagrams over the site analysis, a design concept diagram is derived, character sketches are added, and a program statement is written. After studying the overall context of the project and getting feedback from the developer, a rectilinear design approach is chosen (fig. 9-64). Finally, a section-elevation perspective and sketch are done, and the design process of the urban courtyard is completed.

+ *Good access to shopping center.*

+ *Private space located away from Main Street.*

− *Access to restaurant is through private space.*

− *Public space isn't accessible to parking & sidewalk.*

− *Major circulation is through semi-private space.*

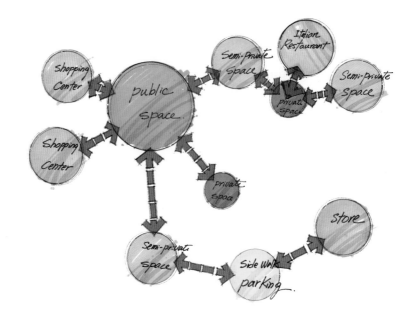

+ *Good access to shopping center.*

+ *Private space located away from Main Street.*

+ *Access to restaurant is through semi-private space.*

+ *Good access from public space to parking & sidewalk.*

+ *Major circulation is through public space.*

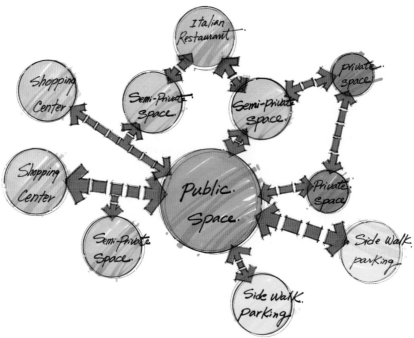

Figure 9-62.

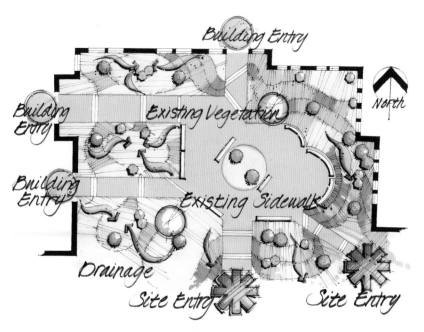

Building Entry

Existing Vegetation

Building Entry

Building Entry

Existing Sidewalk

North

Drainage

Site Entry **Site Entry**

Site inventory

Provide Human Scale

Round form conflicts w/building

North

Needs focal Point

Black out noise and View of parking   Keep view open   Keep Summer Breezes

Site analysis

Overstory Trees

Match Building with Rectilinear forms

North

Focal Point

Vegetation Screen

Low plants to allow views and breezes

Concept Diagram

---

1. Create an exciting place to work, shop and dine.
2. Allow good visibility to all lower level shops.
3. Maintain historical character.
4. Use grade changes to separate different spaces & add interest.
5. Provide open space for use by venders and outdoor entertainment.
6. Provide a focal point to draw people into the space.
7. Use vegetation to articulate and separate spaces.
8. Provide overstory vegetation to create a sense of human scale
9. Create a space that leaves the visiter with lasting memories.

Program statement

Character Sketch

Figure 9-63.

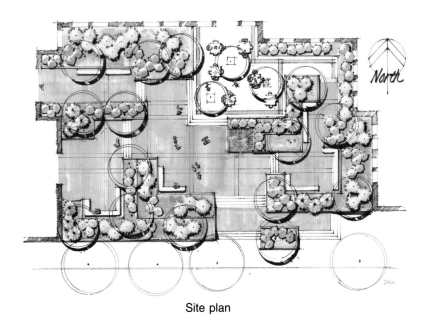

Site plan

Sketch

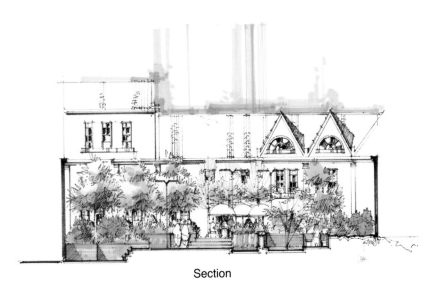

Section

Perspective

Figure 9-64.

APPENDIX A: TIME-SAVING TECHNIQUES

Investments of time and money while drawing and designing can prove costly to both students and professionals alike. Using common sense and some of the following techniques can improve the quality of your presentation and help you save valuable time:

• When constructing a perspective, place a thumbtack at the vanishing point(s) to allow the T-square to swing while drawing lines toward that vanishing point.

• Use commercially made pounce for waxy surfaces such as mylar and vellum, to avoid ink skips when drafting.

• Place a reducing lens (available at optical stores) above the drawing to reduce the size of the drawing and to study the overall value, and use an enlarging lens to do specific detailing.

• Many copy machines now have enlarging and reducing functions, making it especially easy to enlarge and reduce a drawing. If you photograph your work you can also have it enlarged or reduced photographically.

• To rough out a sketch, trace from slides, use diazo prints from slides, or perspective charts. These can be used in place of the more complicated office method.

• Trace the project on a window facing the light source if a light table is not available.

• A quick way to produce an outdoor perspective is to draw with an acetate overlay affixed to a car window. To avoid distortion, this should be done with one eye closed.

• When drawing and doing perspectives, trace people, block out furniture and cars, and imitate vegetation and other entourage.

• Large letters may be traced from press-on lettering sheets to create block letters. This can be particularly useful for title blocks.

• Use templates for circles, ovals, and other shapes where appropriate.

• Use the straight edge of a surface such as a drawing table or even a book to guide your hand when drawing straight lines. By placing your finger on the edge of the object and sliding down, a straight line parallel to the edge is achieved.

• Use a triangle to stop line strokes and a piece of scrap paper over your work sheet to start line strokes where needed. This will create a smooth, crisp edge.

• Use a toothbrush to produce a dot texture on a drawing. Load the toothbrush with wet media and pull across the bristles with your finger.

• To draw texture for grass, ground cover, or carpet, tape two triangles together with the desired spacing, and draw strokes in between.

• Use photo tape, black drafting tape, or zip tape on vellum or mylar for a project border and title block. Avoid the use of marker medium for borders as it tends to bleed and fade to yellow with age.

• Use drafting tape to remove press-on letters if necessary; this avoids tearing the sheet.

• To create different values when making a diazo print, add paper to or cut from original vellum, sepia, or mylar before printing.

• To merge two separate sheets together seamlessly, overlap the sheets as desired, cut through both with one cut, and join the cut edges together with transparent tape applied to the back.

• Layout title blocks on acetate, mylar, or separate printed sepia, and make as many copies as you need to eliminate having to construct the same title block for several sheets.

• Use cut-and-paste or Pelican graphic white to delete mistakes instead of redrawing the entire project.

• Use the dimensions of the elements of your body (hand, height, stride) as a guide to measure the physical site when no tape is available.

• Create drawing files of good examples such as people, cars, trees, etc., as a reference to assist you in drawing and designing.

APPENDIX B: MODEL MATERIALS

$\frac{1}{32}'' = 1'\text{-}0''$	$1'' = 10'\text{-}0''$	$1'' = 100'\text{-}0''$
$\frac{1}{16}'' = 1'\text{-}0''$	$1'' = 20'\text{-}0''$	$1'' = 200'\text{-}0''$
$\frac{1}{8}'' = 1'\text{-}0''$	$1'' = 30'\text{-}0''$	$1'' = 500'\text{-}0''$
$\frac{1}{4}'' = 1'\text{-}0''$	$1'' = 40'\text{-}0''$	$1'' = 1000'\text{-}0''$
$\frac{1}{2}'' = 1'\text{-}0''$	$1'' = 50'\text{-}0''$	

ADHESIVE: Elmer's glue, wood glue, rubber cement, adhesive spray, hot glue gun, glue stick, staples.

BASE: plywood, sheet rock, styrofoam board, celotex, masonite, particle board.

CONTOURS/TOPOGRAPHY: cork sheets, corrugated cardboard, chipboard, styroboard, illustration board, construction paper, foamcore.

TITLE BLOCK: 3-D cardboard letters or plastic letters; press-on letters (black or white).

CARS: commercially bought (toy hobby stores), cardboard, balsa wood, styrofoam.

FIGURES: cut-out silhouette from cardboard; carved from balsa wood, aluminum foil, wire, pins, tacks, or nails; commercially bought; cut from magazine.

BUILDING MASS: chipboard, mat board or cardboard; balsa wood, pine; clay, glass, sugar cubes, foam.

BUILDING WALLS: balsa wood, cardboard, styroboard, facade with xerox or blueprint.

BUILDING ROOFS: sandpaper, balsa wood shingles, sand, cardboard, layout paper.

BUILDING WINDOWS: clear or colored acetate, glass, scratched acetate.

INTERIOR WALLS: scored balsa wood, mat board, illustration board.

INTERIOR FLOORINGS: fabric, delineated chipboard.

INTERIOR BATH FIXTURES: plaster of paris, balsa wood.

INTERIOR FURNITURE: velour ribbon, clay, fabric with wire, cork, balsa wood.

PAVING: natural stone, paint, cork, sandpaper, mat board, construction paper.

STREET LIGHTS: balsa wood, pin heads.

STREET BENCHES: balsa wood, mat board.

TREES AND SHRUBS: yarrow (individual, clusters, structured); foam rubber (fine, medium, and coarse texture); wire cable ($\frac{1}{8}$ inch diam.–$\frac{1}{2}$ inch diam.); yarrow with blooms removed; twigs or wire trees covered with steel wool, foam, sawdust, or lichen; lichen, styrofoam, or papier-mâché.

GROUND COVERS: lichen (fine), cork, ground-up foam rubber, sand and pebbles, coffee grounds or sawdust, paint and spray textures.

GRASS: paint, commercial grass, construction paper.

WATER FOR LAKE, POOL, OR RIVER: blue ziptone, built-up layers with blue or clear acetate, blue paint covered with polymer gloss medium, rough textured glass, liquid resin.

WATER FOR FOUNTAIN: twisted or formed cotton, silver wire, wax, liquid resin, rubber cement.

WATER FOR RAPIDS AND WATERFALL: cotton or wax, rough textured paint.

SCULPTURE: thin wire, paper clips, match sticks, clay, bronze cast, washer, wax, cuttlefish, aluminum foil, beads and pick.

Appendix C: Drawing Paper and Boards

Types of Paper

acetate and frosted acetate
bond paper
buff paper
card stock
charcoal paper
colored bond paper
colored parchment paper
construction paper
craft paper
designer paper
diazo print paper
duplicator paper
engineering layout paper
felt paper
graphite paper
Hypropaper
marker paper
mat
oatmeal paper
pastel paper
photomural paper
poster paper
print-making paper
rice paper
sketch paper/pad
tracing vellum
trash/bumwad paper
watercolor paper
Xerox paper

Types of Board

Bainbridge 172 board
cardboard
chipboard
foamboard
illustration board
mat board
poster board
watercolor board

Paper for Pencil Rendering

bristol pad (vellum finish)
bond paper by Hammermill
illustration board (172) by Bainbridge
print paper
sketch pad by Artworthy
sketch pad (All Techniques) by Grumbacher
sketch paper/pad
Xerox paper

Paper for Pastel Rendering

charcoal paper by Strathmore
fine tooth watercolor paper
yellow tracing paper

Paper for Ink Rendering

bond paper by Hammermill
bristol pad (plate finish) by Grumbacher or Bee
detail paper by Teledyen and Bee
frosted acetate
layout bond by Bee
print paper
sketch pad by Artworthy
vellum or Mylar

Paper for Marker Rendering

bumwad or trash paper
craft board or cardboard
diazo print paper
Hypropaper by Grumbacher
illustration board
marker paper (#638) by Aquabee
marker paper (Graphics) by Bienfang
marker paper by National

Paper for Watercolor Rendering

D'Arches paper by Winsor Newton
watercolor board by Crescent
watercolor paper by Grumbacher or Strathmore

Paper for Tempera Rendering

crescent mat board
crescent 100 illustration board
watercolor board

Paper for Airbrush Rendering

bristol pad (plate finish) by Grumbacher or Bee
Crescent 100 illustration board
layout bond by Bee

APPENDIX D: RECOMMENDED MARKERS LIST

Color	Chartpak AD Marker	Berol Prismacolor Art Marker	Eberhard Faber Design Art Marker	Eberhard Faber Design 2 Art Marker
Warm Grey	Colorless Blender (P-0) Warm Grey #1 (P191) Warm Grey #3 (P193) Warm Grey #5 (P195) Warm Grey #7 (P197) Black (P98)	Blender (PM-121) French Gray 20% (PM-156) French Gray 40% (PM-158) French Gray 60% (PM-160) French Gray 80% (PM-162) Black (PM-98)	Colorless Blender (311) Warm Grey-2 (209-L2) Warm Grey-4 (209-L4) Warm Grey-6 (209-L6) Warm Grey-8 (209-L8) Black (229-L)	Colorless Blender Warm Grey V.2 (Warm Grey 2) Warm Grey V.4 (Warm Grey 4) Warm Grey V.6 (Warm Grey 6) Warm Grey V.8 (Warm Grey 8) Black (Black)
Blue	Sapphire Blue (P107) Ice Blue (P105) Crystal Blue (P108) Electric Blue (P102) Prussian Blue (P6)	Light Cerulean Blue (PM-48) Mediterranean Blue (PM-143) True Blue (PM-40) Copenhagen Blue (PM-43)	Blue–0 (265-L0) Blue–1 (265-L1) Peacock (425-L) Blue–9 (265-L9)	Turquoise V.1 (Pale Turquoise) Turquoise V.2 (Aqua) Turquoise V.3 (Turquoise) Turquoise V.4 (Peacock Blue) Turquoise V.5 (Indigo Blue)
Blue Green	Pale Lime (P118) Turquoise Green (P115) Aqua (P117) Slate Green (P18) Deep Evergreen (P219)	Deco Green (PM-135) Light Aqua (PM-46) Aquamarine (PM-37) Peacock Blue (PM-125)	Blue Green–0 (205-L0) Blue Green–1 (205-L1) Blue Green (205-L) Blue Green–9 (205-L9)	Blue Green V.1 (Pale Blue Green) Blue Green V.2 (Mint) Blue Green V.3 (Blue Green) Blue Green V.4 (Viridian) Blue Green V.5 (Evergreen)
Olive Green	Maize (P133) Pale Olive (P34) Olive (P31) Dark Olive (P24)	Not Available	Pale Ivy (488-L) Green Or. Green (248-L) Green Or. Green–9 (248-L9)	Olive V.1 (Pale Olive) Olive V.2 (Willow) Olive V.3 (Olive) Olive V.4 (Olive Drab) Olive V.5 (Sap Green)
Yellow Green	Celery (P126) Linden Green (P37) Palm Green (P32) Emerald Green (P21) Willow Green (P120) Apple Green (P28) Jade (P25)	Cream (PM-23) Deco Yellow (PM-131) Chartreuse (PM-27) Apple Green (PM-167) Olive Green (PM-28)	Yellow Green–1 (208-L1) Willow (478-L) Apple Green (448-L)	Yellow Green V.1 (Pale Yel. Gre) Yellow Green V.2 (Celery Green) Yellow Green V.3 (Yellow Green) Yellow Green V.4 (Moss Green) Yellow Green V.5 (Chrome Green)
Yellow Brown	Cream (P132) Goldenrod (P46) Pale Sepia (P50) Sepia (P56) Redwood (P69)	Blondwood (PM-96) Jasmine (PM-132) Yellow Ochre (PM-69) Light Umber (PM-172)	Yellow (257-L) Yellow Orange (207-L) Yellow Brown (233-L) Red Brown (213—L)	Yellow Orange V.1 (Pale Yel. Ora.) Yellow Orange V.2 (Light Pumpkin) Yellow Orange V.3 (Yellow Orange) Yellow Orange V.4 (Indian Yellow) Yellow Orange V.5 (Brown Ochre)
Brown	Light Sand (P138) Suntan (P140) Mocha (P70) Burnt Umber (P71) Delta Brown (P57)	Brick Beige (PM-78) Sand (PM-70) Dark Brown (PM-88)	Buff (433-L) Raw Wood (283-L) Pale Walnut (273-L) Walnut (263-L) Dark Oiled Walnut (393-L)	Buff Putty Light Walnut Van Dyke Brown Walnut
Red Brown	Flesh (P149) Peach (P153) Brick Red (P74) Burnt Sienna (P75) Maroon (P85)	Light Peach (PM-12) Cherry (PM-86) Tuscan Red (PM-169)	Brown–0 (293-L0) Brown–1 (293-L1) Pale Mahogany (353-L) Mahogany (343-L) Red Brown–9 (213-L9)	Buff Sand Kraft Red Wood Chocolate
Red	Powder Pink (P161) Salmon (P160) Deep Salmon (P206) Scarlet (P81) Ruby (P83)	Blush (PM-10) Carmine Red (PM-6) Crimson Red (PM-4) Raspberry (PM-151) Mahogany Red (PM-150)	Red–0 (336-L0) Red–1 (336-L1) Red–8 (336-L8) Red–9 (336-L9)	Red V.1 (Pale Pink) Red V.2 (Pink) Red V.3 (Red) Red V.4 (Crimson) Red V.5 (Maroon)
Violet	Mauve (P177) Bright Orchid (P209) Lilac (P92) Purple Iris (P210) Violet (P94)	Deco Pink (PM-133) Lavender (PM-59) Dahlia Purple (PM-129) Dark Purple (PM-168)	Mauve (434-L) Pale Purple (424-L) Violet (254-L)	Violet V.1 (Pale Violet) Violet V.2 (Lilac) Violet V.3 (Violet) Violet V.4 (Royal Purple) Violet V.5 (Grape)

REFERENCES

ENTOURAGE

Burden, Ernest. *Entourage: A Tracing File for Architecture and Interior Design Drawing.* New York: McGraw-Hill, 1981.

Evans, Larry. *Illustration Guide.* New York: Van Nostrand Reinhold, 1982.

PLAN, SECTION, ELEVATION

Walker, Theodore D. *Plan Graphics.* New York: Van Nostrand Reinhold, 1988.

Wang, Thomas C. *Plan and Section Drawing.* New York: Van Nostrand Reinhold, 1979.

RENDERING TECHNIQUES

Atkins, William. *Architectural Presentation Techniques.* New York: Van Nostrand Reinhold, 1976.

Calle, Paul. *The Pencil.* New York: Watson-Guptill, 1974.

Doyle, Michael E. *Color Drawing: A Marker-Colored-Pencil Approach.* New York: Van Nostrand Reinhold, 1981.

Drpic, Ivo D. *Architectural Delineation: Professional Shortcuts.* New York: Van Nostrand Reinhold, 1988.

Dudley, Levitt. *Architectural Illustration.* New York: McGraw-Hill, 1977.

Edwards, Betty. *Drawing on the Right Side of the Brain,* 2d ed. Los Angeles: Tarcher, 1989.

Halse, Albert O. *Architectural Rendering: The Technique of Contemporary Presentation,* 2d ed. New York: McGraw-Hill, 1972.

Kautzky, Ted. *The Ted Kautzky Pencil Book.* New York: Van Nostrand Reinhold, 1979.

Kautzky, Ted. *Ways with Watercolor,* 2d ed. New York: Van Nostrand Reinhold, 1963.

Leach, Sid Delmar. *Techniques of Interior Design Rendering and Presentation.* New York: McGraw-Hill, 1978.

Linton, Harold and Roy Strickfaden. *Architectural Sketching in Markers.* New York: Van Nostrand Reinhold, 1991.

Oles, Steve. *Architectural Illustration.* New York: Van Nostrand Reinhold, 1979.

Oliver, Robert. *The Complete Sketches.* New York: Van Nostrand Reinhold, 1989.

Reid, Grant. *Landscape Graphics.* New York: Whitney, 1987.

Wang, Thomas C. *Pencil Sketching.* New York: Van Nostrand Reinhold, 1977.

Wang, Thomas C. *Sketching with Markers.* New York: Van Nostrand Reinhold, 1981.

RENDERING EXAMPLES

Burden, Ernest. *Architectural Delineation.* New York: McGraw-Hill, 1982.

Jacoby, Helmut. *New Architectural Drawings.* New York: Praeger, 1969.

Kemper, Alfred M. *Presentation Drawings by American Architects.* New York: John Wiley & Sons, 1977.

Lin, Mike. *Architectural Rendering Techniques: A Color Reference.* New York: Van Nostrand Reinhold, 1985.

Walker, Theodore D. *Perspective Sketches,* 5th ed. New York: Van Nostrand Reinhold, 1989.

DESIGN

Baker, Geoffrey. Design Strategies in Architecture, *An Approach to the Analysis of Form.* New York: Van Nostrand Reinhold (International), 1989.

Clark, Roger and Michael Pause. *Precedents in Architecture.* New York: Van Nostrand Reinhold, 1985.

Friedmann, Arnold, John Pile and Forrest Wilson. *Interior Design, An Introduction to Architectural Interiors,* 3d ed., New York: Elsevier, 1982.

Molnar, Donald J. et al. *Anatomy of a Park,* 2d ed., New York: McGraw Hill, 1986.

Simonds, John O. Landscape Architecture: A Manual of Site Planning and Design. New York: McGraw-Hill, 1983. rev. ed.

CREDITS

ILLUSTRATION CREDITS: The following are firms that generously contributed drawings of their various projects. I extend my deep appreciation to them, for without their contributions, this book would not have had the variety and the quality that make it so unique and useful.

Art Associates, Toledo, OH

Belt, Collins, and Associates, Honolulu, HI

Bloodgood Architects, Inc., Des Moines, IA

Communication Arts, Boulder, CO

EDAW, Fort Collins, CO

Howard, Needles, Tammen, and Bergendoff, Kansas City, MO

Johnson, Johnson, and Roy, Inc., Ann Arbor, MI

Fay Jones and Maurice Jennings Architects, Fayetteville, AK

Land Design/Research, Inc., Columbia, MD

Lockwood Greene Engineers, Inc., Spartanburg, SC

Gary Mellenbruch, Kansas City, MO

Craig Patterson and Associates, Kansas City, MO

Point Line Graphics, Inc., Middleton, WI

Prelim and Associates, Dallas, TX

RTKL Associates Inc., Baltimore, MD

Dick Sneary and Associates, Kansas City, MO

Edward D. Stone, Jr. and Associates, Ft. Lauderdale, FL

CONCEPTS CREDITS: I would like to extend my gratitude to the people I met both in my workshops in Kansas and on my travel tours. These people have either contributed their findings or given concepts support in this book: Betty Edwards (right brain and left brain), Gail Gunter (paraline drawing), Robert Hanna (transfer image), Allen Hastings (marker technical tips—cardboard strip), Donald Molnar and Albert Rutledge (a case study in design process), Sharon Nielsen (color pair), Herbert Schaal (proportional method), John Silva (circle in perspective: method two), and Tracy Zachos (figure and face).

CONCEPTS SUPPORT

Alexandria Technical Institute: Candace Johnson. Arizona State University: David Di Cicco, Mike Evans, Bob Wolf. Auburn University: Brian LaHaie. Ball State University: Scott Collard. California Polytechnic State University-Pomona: Ken Nakaba. California Polytechnic State University-San Luis Obispo: Alice Loh, Larry Loh, Gerald Smith, Richard Zweifel. Clemson University: Faculty. Colorado State University: Merlyn Paulson, Grant Reid. Conway School of Landscape Design: Walt Cudnohufsky. Cornell University: Marvin Adleman. Drury College: Faculty. Endacott College: Allen Dunphy. Florida International University: John Sanderson. Harvard University: Charles Harris. Iowa State University: Paul Anderson, Gina Crandell, Mira Engler. Kansas State University: Faculty. Lawrence Technological University: Faculty. Louisiana State University: Van Cox, Neil Odenwald, Sieshiro Tomioka. Massachusetts Institute of Technology: Faculty. Meramec College: Kay Hagan. Michigan State University: Anthony Bauer. Milwaukee Area Technical College: John Schaefgen, James Walczak. Mississippi State University: Calvin Bishop, Cameron Man, Charles Parks. Morgan State University: Ken Trionfo. North Carolina A & T State University: Ronnie Bailey, John Robinson. North Carolina State University: Faculty. North Dakota State University: Faculty. Ohio State University: Jot Carpenter, James Hiss. Oklahoma State University: Paul Hsu, Charles Leider. Pennsylvania State University: Neil Porterfield. Purdue University: Philip DeTurk, Donald Molnar, Greg Pierceall. Rhode Island School of Design: Faculty. Rutgers University: Steven Strom, John and Constance Webster. San Jose State University: Faculty. South Dakota State University: Faculty. Southwest Missouri State University: Stephanie Gustine, Tom Kachel. Southern Illinois University at Carbondale: Norm Lach. State University of New York at Cobleskill: Jack Ingels. State University of New York at Syracuse: Faculty. Texas A & M University: Faculty. Texas Tech University: Jean Kavanagh, Robert Marlett, James Mertes, Tom Musiak. Triton College: John Silva. University of Arizona: Michael Deeter, Kirby Lockard. University of Arkansas: Martha and Cyrus Sutherland. University of British Columbia: Patrick Mooney. University of California at Berkeley: Faculty. University of Colorado at Denver: Faculty. University of Florida: Lester Linscott, Herrick Smith. James Winebrenner. University of Georgia: Gregg Coyle, Marguerite Koepke, Julie Myers. University of Guelph: Faculty. University of Hawaii: Faculty. University of Idaho: Faculty. University of Illinois: Natalie Alpert. University of Kansas: Steve Pedget. University of Kentucky: Janice Cervelli, Horst Schach. University of Massachusetts: Nicholas Dines, Ann Marston. University of Minnesota: Roger Martin, Peter Olin. University of Missouri: Dick Melmick. University of Montreal: Faculty. University of Nebraska: Robert Duncan. University of Oklahoma: Georgia Muenzler, Raymond Yeh. University of Rhode Island: Richard Hanson, Angelo Simeoni. University of Pennsylvania: Ian McHarg. University of Texas at Arlington: Randle Harwood, Gary Robinette. University of Toronto: John Consolati. University of Virginia: Harry Porter. University of Washington: Faculty. University of Wisconsin at Madison: Charles Law, Philip Lewis. University of Wisconsin at Stout: Faculty. Utah State University: Larry Wegkamp. Virginia Polytechnic Institute and State University: Faculty. Washington State University: Wayne Williams. West Virginia University: Cliff Collier, George Longnecker, Alan Kvashny.

INDEX